THE PINEAP

The PINEAPPLE TART

ANNE DUNLOP

POOLBEG

A paperback original
First published 1992 by
Poolbeg Press Ltd
Knocksedan House,
Swords, Co Dublin, Ireland

Reprinted November 1994

The financial assistance of the Arts Council of Northern Ireland is gratefully
acknowledged

ISBN 1 85371 405 4

Cover illustration and design by Wendy Robinson
Set by Richard Parfrey in Stone Serif 10/15
Printed and bound in Great Britain by
Cox & Wyman Ltd, Reading, Berkshire

Anne Dunlop was born in Castledawson Co Derry Northern Ireland in 1968. She graduated in Agricultural Science at University College Dublin in 1991 and then returned to Northern Ireland to do postgraduate work. *The Pineapple Tart* is her first novel.

To my mother and father

CHAPTER ONE

The Very Reverend Roger Simms, who had bored us witless for years in church, was suddenly called to the Mission Fields and the Reverend Adam Robinson was called to fill the post. The day he visited to introduce himself is poignantly memorable. Jennifer had tried to dye her hair red and had succeeded in dyeing her ears and the back of her neck as well, and mummy and daddy weren't speaking to each other because mummy had burned yesterday's newspaper and daddy hadn't finished the crossword in it.

Daddy was sulking because he had lain awake half the night trying to think of "An aniseed-flavoured liqueur" and when inspiration had hit him the next morning as he was ploughing, he had abandoned the tractor mid-furrow and run the whole way up to the house to fill in the answer.

Finding that the paper had been used to light the range and mummy consoling Jennifer that the dye was not permanent and would wear away in about six weeks, he had thrown a classic wobbly, the type that made Jennifer's wobblies look like indigestion. So mummy sulked because daddy sulked, and Jennifer sulked because we all laughed at her ears; and Adam arrived in the midst of the sulking tumult, and I had to entertain him because Laura fell in love with him the moment she clapped eyes on him and couldn't speak. I am sure Adam thought us a very strange family. You see mummy and daddy are incapable of rational behaviour when they are sulking. Daddy had locked himself in the outside loo, which is, he claims, the only place he can find peace, and mummy had driven off in a cloud of smoke to visit Ruth Paisley, the one woman in the world daddy detests, because she knew it would make him crosser. Daddy hates Ruth because she was originally married to his friend Johnny but deserted him after thirteen years because he pulled the bedclothes off her in the middle of the night and cut himself shaving. She had promptly acquired a toy-boy called Sid, who wore white socks and picked his nose when he was nervous. He appeared to be nervous a lot. Daddy always claimed that Ruth put feminist thoughts into mummy's head. I can't agree. I think they were always there.

Daisy embarrassed us terribly by offering to make tea, floating off and not coming back. It seems that *en route* to the kitchen she forgot what she was going there for and took off with Brenda her terrier for a walk instead. We had no biscuits to offer Adam, so he got a banana with his tea. Incidentally, we had no tea either but I retrieved a tea-bag from the bin and washed it carefully under the tap before putting it in the teapot. Mummy wasn't noted for her stupendous housekeeping, and frequently we ran short on such essentials as tea-bags and soft loo-roll.

We have a pile of newspapers in the outside loo for emergency situations, and when daddy escaped there, he invariably reread the news from weeks or even months before.

When Adam left, Laura clutched her left breast and fell groaning to the floor. I thought she had had a heart attack and dashed over to administer first aid.

"He is the one," she whispered dramatically. "He is the man for me." She spent the night in a wardrobe in an attic which was where she retreated when she had to be alone.

Next day in church we discovered Adam's wife Rachael and their two daughters Patience and Hope. They were a very wet family.

"Not much beef on her," daddy remarked at lunch. He and mummy had made up sometime during the night. They were grinning idiotically at each other over the stew. As they clasped each other's hands daddy added, "A man wants a woman he can hold on to."

Now, subjectively speaking, I do not think that Laura would make a minister's wife if she lived to be a hundred. Ministers' wives should be sincere, plain and obedient; they should care for the well-being of others; they should be the doormats of the congregation. They should organise cake sales and charity collections. They should have no "sins of the flesh" or "worldly leanings." Laura didn't fit any of these categories. If there was any bad to be done Laura did it.

There was one day when we were fourteen and fifteen when she decided she wanted to be drunk, and invited me along to drink a bottle of brandy with her. She sold her book-token—a Sunday school prize— to buy the bottle. She had got the top prize for memorising Isaiah 53. The book-token was valuable because we didn't get pocket money—bad for children, my parents said.

We started drinking in the attic wardrobe after Saturday lunch because Laura felt we needed the entire afternoon: we might get "overhangs" and we had to have recovered before dinner. I can't say I appreciated the burn as I swallowed the first mouthful but once started we didn't stop. Gordons don't start a thing and then give up. The brandy warmed all my organs, in fact I was sure my toes were curling in the heat. Laura said she could feel her fingernails growing. A few more mouthfuls and suddenly there were two Lauras. Everything she said caused me to collapse in helpless giggles. I felt as if I had a huge bubble inside my head and I was so light I could float. Laura was swimming breast stroke along the dusty floor and I was barking like a dog when mummy caught us.

Laura promptly stopped swimming, sat bolt upright and vomited rings round her. There seemed to be carrots everywhere, and I was sure we had no carrots for lunch. In the deadly silence that followed I hiccuped really loudly but nobody laughed. We were dosed with a pint glass each of Andrews Liver Salts.

"Drink it when it's fizzing," mummy said. "It's no good unless it's fizzing."

We were put to bed to await our hangovers and our punishment when daddy came in for tea and I lay quaking in case he would shout at me. The drunkenness had worn off and a blinding headache had begun.

I crept into the adjoining room to see if Laura was living or dead. She was fast asleep snoring like a pig. My head ached worse listening to her.

I decided to apologise immediately to daddy—lying in bed waiting for him to punish me was worse than the real thing. So I crept down the stairs and to the door of the sitting room, where I knew mummy was watching *The Quiet Man,* one of her two favourite films. The other was *Gone with the Wind* and she had both videotaped. We watched them both about once every couple of weeks. I was madly in love with Rhett Butler from the start. Laura always preferred Shaun Thornton: she said it was the American twang that turned her on. And it helped that he was kinda broad at the shoulder and slim at the hip. Daisy much preferred Ashley because he was "sensitive," she said. She wanted a man who understood the rhythm of the sea. All Sarah asked was that her man had no hairs on his toes.

Daddy was in the sitting room with mummy and he was laughing.

"The little menaces," he said over and over again. I crept back up stairs. The spanking I received is one I have never forgotten, and I was spanked frequently as a child. Around the same age I caught Laura smoking in the wardrobe. I thought her perfectly wonderful as I simply could not inhale. I tried and tried and Laura tried and tried to teach me but it was useless. I always choked at the critical moment when smoke tickled the back of my throat. So she stopped smoking because she said it was no fun being bad alone. How could a wild thing like Laura marry Adam Robinson? Just supposing Rachael disappeared from the paths of this world to take her place among the righteous of the next. Adam was old: he was at least thirty and he wasn't even handsome. Even Daisy with all her daft ideas wanted a young man.

After she met Adam Laura revised the entire situation. She forgot about Shaun Thornton and took to religion. Originally she had been the heathen among us, the one who coaxed Daisy and me into spending our church collection on sweets. The plan had worked brilliantly up to the point where Daisy absent-mindedly put her packet of Polo mints on the collection plate. Daddy had intercepted the plate and the Polos and we were spanked with a high-heeled shoe that day. Particularly painful. Usually daddy cut a young ash plant from the hedge for a major beating, but it had been raining that day and he had a hole in his Sunday shoes.

Laura began to attend the Sunday evening services and the prayer meeting on a Thursday night. It meant that someone had to drive her into church and that she missed *Top of the Pops* but she considered such loss her gain. I asked what she prayed about. She said that she asked God to make Rachael run away with the postman and to let Adam fall in love with her. She wasn't wicked enough to pray that Rachael die, simply that she would disappear without trace and without memory.

"He must be a wonderful lover," she mooned one

day while we were gathering potatoes. "He has such latent sexual tension. Don't be deceived by that mousy appearance, girls. Passion glows from his eyes. Oh for the steadiness of that heart and the timbre of that voice."

Sarah had been shocked. "Ministers procreate," she said. "They don't make love." If Sarah hadn't been so outrageously beautiful we would have hated her. She even tanned in the sun while the rest of us burned, peeled and stank of brown vinegar. Mummy said Sarah was a "nice" girl and secretly we would have all happily been "nice" girls if we could have been half as beautiful.

All except Jennifer who considered herself quite as beautiful as Sarah. I don't know why she thought that. She had the same pale freckled skin as the rest of us and the same snub nose as Laura. But she had neither Laura's cleavage nor Daisy's long legs. She couldn't rival my small ears and symmetrical eyebrows so she was really the runt of the litter. Laura cried for three solid days when she heard that Rachael was expecting another baby. Mummy became worried and gave her the "What's the matter with you?" talk. Laura said her heart was broken and mummy said she had never heard anything so ridiculous—Laura was too young to have a heart. I was no help because I had never been in love and Daisy was even vaguer than usual.

"To produce for a man the image and seed of himself must be the ultimate gift a woman can offer, after herself."

With the resilience of youth Laura soon came round.

"What did I ever see in him?" she wailed. "He's boring and wet and a *minister*." She gave up religion and started swearing under her breath again, a habit she had given up when she took up prayer meetings. Mummy was rather relieved.

"It was enjoyable to have her religious for that short time," she said, "but really, she isn't the religious type. I don't think she was sent to earth to be a saint." Laura and Rev Robinson was the foretaste of love for us, the Gordons. None of us forgot it. And none of us married a minister.

CHAPTER TWO

Mummy, who is big into the education of her daughters, was delighted when I got accepted to study agricultural science at college in Dublin. Daddy wasn't so pleased because he considered intelligence in a woman secondary to all her other attributes. He was foolish enough to tell me too in front of mummy:

"I wouldn't have married your mother if she had been smart," and mummy had huffed for a week and got her hair cut up really short to spite him. (He loathes women with short hair.) She looked like a prisoner of war, or a cancer victim when she returned from the hairdressers and having bit off her nose to spite her face she retired to bed to cry her eyes out. Mummy is terribly impulsive.

Laura had disgraced herself the year before by failing all her A Levels. It wasn't that she wasn't smart—she could have bought and sold her granny—but that she had spent a lot of time visiting "Kate" over the year. Frequently, too frequently her exam results would suggest, a car load of Laura's mates arrived for her and took her off to "Kate's." Mummy thought Kate was a bedridden friend; she was in fact the only pub in the district which sold drink to the under-aged. I had been persuaded to accompany her once but had felt so guilty at actually being in a public house I hadn't gone again. Laura drank vodka and something because she said that you couldn't smell vodka off someone's breath. I think she would have drunk anything you bought her. Mummy remained oblivious to this decadent behaviour because Laura sucked-in before kissing her *en route* to bed. Anyway, daddy thought the sun shone out of Laura's eyes, and she was so sly our parents never suspected her capable of deceit or dishonesty.

"I loath intellect," she would moan while we studied for our exams, me for my first attempt, she for her second.

We had originally studied in our respective bedrooms but Laura's room had no fireplace, and she complained that she was so cold her brain froze over and she couldn't concentrate. Then she would join me in my room and sigh and fidget and rustle paper so that I couldn't concentrate. And when I refused to talk to her, she would tease Henry the terrier, who lived at the bottom of my bed. He bit her once when she pulled his tail and she bit him back again. Usually though she did manage to distract me and we'd end up painting each other's faces and practising hairstyles on each other's heads. Personally I found it far harder to blend blusher so I didn't look like a Sioux warrior than I did to study maths. I told mummy once, when she caught Laura plucking my eyebrows, "It's only curve-sketching mummy; I can curve sketches."

I had discovered boys when I was sixteen. Perhaps they had discovered me. I'm not sure but what ever the way it was it's been mutual admiration ever since. I altered my school skirt up and in: I carried lipgloss in my pencil case and spot concealer in the pocket of my duffel coat. There was little I could do about the duffel coat, which had tartan lining, but it was better than Laura's, which had white fur.

I stopped combing my hair because I thought I looked sexy with it ruffled round my face. Laura's interest was, I believe, more enthusiastic than elemental but she copied me the day I drew my face shape on the mirror to discover whether it was round, square or long. I'm still not sure.

"Mummy says you have sex appeal," said Sarah. "She says it's not your fault." Sarah thought "sex appeal" was a dirty word.

Laura probably benefited more from our sessions than me because I was interested in her English course and we would talk about the novels she was studying. Usually I read them and told her what they were about. I thought *Wuthering Heights* the most passionate book and cried for days after reading it. Laura's reaction to the tragedy I always thought epitomised her attitude to life:

"Well I think they are awful idiots to get so worked up over each other. I bet Cathy wasn't even good-looking."

There were slaps and tears when I announced my intention to study in Dublin.

"Dublin!" Daddy spat the word out as if it caused a bad taste in his mouth. "What would you want to live in that bastion of popery for?" He was furious when he heard that Laura his pet was going there too. All that irked him of course was the slagging his Orange friends would give him and to such prejudice I paid little heed.

Laura didn't actually want to study in Dublin as she had heard that the drink was very expensive but she wasn't prepared to go to England without me.

"It wouldn't be the same," she pouted dismally when I informed her that my mind was made up about Dublin. "Why can't you make up your mind to go to England instead? Everyone who went there from my class says it's a great place—we could be real cool trendy students." She pictured herself wearing black clothes and white make-up, dyeing her hair jet and doing drugs. And maybe studying "One Dimensional

Man" or some other obscure arty course. I stuck to
my guns. Dublin was 120 miles away and uncharted
territory for Ulster Presbyterians. When I was in
primary school we had a drawing on the wall of
Northern Ireland with blue surrounding it. I thought
Northern Ireland was an island until I was twelve.
There was less than no chance of us ever meeting a
Presbyterian that we knew, as the percentage of
Presbyterians in University College was probably point
zero something. Anyway, if I was in Dublin I could
discard the trendy student bit and come back to
Derryrose and be Helen again when I wanted. I could
ride Romeo, our fat pony, and sleep with Henry, and
listen to the wind playing hide-and-seek in the orchard
and watch the sun set in the picture window in the
dining room. I could sit at the bedroom window and
listen to daddy talking to himself in the yard below.
I could gossip to Daisy and Sarah and Jennifer and
fight with them over the stupid things that sisters
always fight about. Laura didn't understand any of
this "sentimental drivel" as she called it because she
never thought about anyone but herself but she
recognised the determined Gordon streak in me when
I said that my mind was made up about UCD.

"You mad old eejit," she would say, "Still I suppose
there must be men and sex and wild times in Dublin
too."

Daddy also supposed there were men and sex and wild times in Dublin and took no chances. He correctly reasoned that our, rather Laura's plans would have little chance of development in a Presbyterian hostel and proceeded to enrol us in one such place in the vicinity of the college.

The morning we were to leave I rose at six to cook us breakfast. Mummy and daddy had never been to the South before and were highly suspicious of the natives of the Republic. I had lurid visions of wild-haired women and loads of barefoot children; daddy was convinced the water was poisoned and that we would be stoned.

They consumed Ulster Fries that would have set a field-hand back for a week. Laura thought it was the only thing they had in common. I toyed with a bowl of Branflakes while they gazed into each other's eyes and played footsie under the table. I felt emotional at leaving home and wanted them to pay attention to me and not to each other.

"Did you know," said mummy as she dipped her bread into the yolk of her duck egg, "did you know that your father and I met each other twenty-five years ago today?"

Daddy had parked his brand new Morris on double yellow lines outside the picture-house and mummy's boyfriend—a pasty-faced pipsqueak, daddy says—had scraped the paintwork squeezing past in his car. (Big back seats, mummy said.) The pasty-faced pipsqueak was an honourable young man however and he and mummy waited outside the picture-house until daddy emerged. (He was wearing a navy blazer and looked awfully handsome, mummy said.) The honourable pipsqueak offered to pay for the damage, but daddy took one look at mummy, who is rather pretty, and said not to mind, he would have mummy instead. And so he did, and they were married three months later.

Strangers often wonder what my parents see in each other. Daddy is really anti-social and rude to people he doesn't like. He always thought Rev Simms a pompous windbag and hid in the outside loo when the Rev visited. The one time mummy bribed, bullied and blackmailed him into appearing in the sitting room he tried to fall asleep and when the Rev attempted to include him in the conversation, he mortified everyone by saying, "I don't want to talk to you, I don't like you."

Mummy was so badly annoyed she slept on the sofa for a week. She is much younger than daddy and would be good crack if she wasn't my mother. She is so highly strung that living with her is like April weather, all sunshine and calm one minute, thunder and tears the next. I gave up fussing about her years ago. Daddy thinks she looks beautiful when she's angry.

Daddy was convinced that the Morris—the same Morris of twenty-five years ago—wasn't going to make it to Dublin and was hyperactive as he loaded our bags into the boot. Mummy wasn't allowed to assist but stood by oohing and aahing at the appropriate intervals to encourage him. A tornado wouldn't have blown Emily off the roof-rack of the car, but daddy said that you could never be too careful, a Catholic would steal the eye out of your head and come back for the lash. Emily had belonged to gran-gran and he accorded her heirloom status. Mummy and I tried the tension of the ropes holding her on and made impressed noises to please him. The girls got up to wave us off but we had to turn at the end of the road because mummy had forgotten her knitting pattern and couldn't remember if she was working at the front or the back of the sweater she was knitting daddy for Christmas.

Laura and I were to share a room in the Youth Hostel and we cried and cried when we saw it. Dismal and dusty were the two adjectives I chose, Laura's couldn't be printed. It was fortunate that neither of us noticed the dirt because I don't think that the room was ever cleaned the entire time we were there. I know because I wrote "Helen G. 1st Ag" in the dust the first evening I arrived and it was still there the day we left. Mummy and daddy thought we were crying because they were leaving and kept saying things like:

"We are only a phone call away," or "Don't forget that mummy loves you."

After they left we had dinner of dishwater, chewy wallpaper and apple tart. It transpired that the dishwater was E32 and E45 masquerading as leek and potato soup, and the wallpaper was pretending to be chicken. I gained half a stone by Christmas on the stodge and Laura lost half a stone and swore that if she ever had to eat apple tart again she would kill herself.

We decided after the second day that the chances of being cool trendy students in the hostel were decidedly slim. It appeared however that we couldn't escape. Some forms had been signed and a deposit paid and we were imprisoned there until the summer. The members of our respective faculties were no better. I was surrounded ten-to-one with men, half of whom still smelled of cows and who blushed when I spoke to them. Laura had notably fewer males in the Arts Faculty, and all the girls seemed to be from the city and to wear luminous green which was, I believe, the colour of the season that year. All in all it was a rather unpromising start and I spent the first fortnight in a dream about the dahlias and cooking apples at Derryrose. Laura spent the fortnight complaining that she hated the Dublin accent and that there were no sexpot men to be found. Then I met Richard Knight and Laura shifted Mick Quinlivan in a cupboard at an Ag party and suddenly our attitudes changed. Mick was a mountainous mountain man with huge hands. His relationship with Laura was, she said, purely sexual. This was just as well because our parents would have approved faster of marriage to an Arab than shifting with a Catholic. I considered us much too young for real relationships and went for quantity rather than quality. What had always appealed to me was one man one night and another the next. I had lost count of the number of one-night-shift affairs I had indulged in since I was allowed out dancing. I planned to deal with the quality-control restriction when I was really old, like twenty-two, or twenty-three.

Richard was different. He was my friend because he was the only male in my class impervious to my wiles. When I tried wrapping him round the finger I wrapped the rest around he would simply frown or laugh depending on his mood and tell me to behave. I respected him.

We had met at the bicycle sheds in UCD one windswept October morning when he had offered a piece of bailer twine to tie up Emily—I had forgotten her chain. At the time I thought him rather gruff but when I discovered him reading *Biggles* at the back of a physics lecture the next day I was determined to win him over. He knew that Blake had written "Jerusalem," that *Hamlet* had seven soliloquies, and he took me to hear *The Creation* performed by Trinity Choir. It was the first intellectual relationship I ever had with a man. I don't think Laura liked Richard much, she said you couldn't trust a man who preferred Yeats to *Playboy*, and "Jesu, Joy of Man's Desiring" to Bruce Springsteen. I adored him from the start and was proud of my ability to be friends with one man without the sweet torment of sex between us.

"At least Richard is Protestant," I would chide her when she, jealous of our apparent intimacy, would snidely criticise our friendship.

Still we were happy our first term away from Derryrose and I was only wildly excited and not delirious with joy to be going home for Christmas. Laura didn't want to go back at all. She said Derryrose was insular and our family provincial. She sobbed bitterly the day we left Dublin and it was very embarrassing on the bus. I think the driver thought she was drunk or that I was kidnapping her. He gave me his hanky to dry her eyes and half a packet of Fruit Polos which were fluffy from being inside his jacket pocket. The woman behind us kept patting her hand saying, "It can't be as bad as that love." Perhaps she thought Laura was pregnant.

The minute I got home I went outside to the gardens to hear the silence. The apple trees are older than anyone alive now and the orchard holds the calm of past lives. I touched the tree my great-grandmother grew from seed the year my grandfather was born and sat on a stone pew some ancestor, now dust, had built into the south wall. When I got up, a little stiff and damp, I confess, I was Helen again, Helen from Derryrose—Helen from Dublin cast off with my rucksack.

CHAPTER THREE

That Christmas my parents went through the menopause together. I hope that's what it was—their behaviour wasn't normal, even by their standards. It began the morning mummy decided she had asked daddy one time too often to cut sticks for the range and took the chainsaw to do the job herself. Once she was out of the house I sneaked the key to the lock on the telephone—hidden in the china pot holding the lemon tree—and phoned a girl I had been to school with, now at university in Scotland. Mummy has since taken to disconnecting the telephone and bringing it with her when she leaves the house.

"Helen, Helen!" I heard her screaming for me before she reached the back door, and had hung up, relocked and replaced the key before she made it into the house.

Her right hand was covered in blood, her face panic-stricken.

"I've got to get to the hospital." She was trying to be calm, "I think I'm bleeding to death."

I frantically searched my room for a matching pair of shoes whilst Laura held her arm in the air—to stop the blood running out, she said. Mummy was lying on the tiled floor when I got back downstairs, and Laura, who wouldn't panic if a landmine exploded beneath her, was calmly strapping a bandage onto her arm that she had made from a tea-towel. She was telling mummy that it couldn't be an artery or she would be dead. Mummy, her face pressed to the tiles, wasn't convinced.

I must say that she was so distressed that she didn't complain about my driving once on the way to the hospital. She was busy leaving instructions as to her funeral. The house was to be private, she didn't want artificial flowers, we were to bury her in her grey wool dress as it was so old no one would want to wear it anyway. She didn't want daddy to remarry, but if he did, the new wife wasn't to get any of her jewellery or tea-sets. Anyway, once the panic was over and I was sitting in the hospital waiting for her to be stitched I began feeling a little foolish. Riding-boots look daft with stripy pyjamas, and my mascara was still caked on my face from the night before. I sent up a thankful prayer that Laura had had the wit to pull mummy's wellie boots off and replace them with walking shoes before helping her into the car.

She was fully recovered by the time she reappeared

all smiles because the doctor had made her laugh. But she started using the wrist as an excuse for everything.

We got back from church on Christmas Eve, cold and ravenous, to find her mournfully resting it on a rocking chair in front of the range.

"None of you are getting a bite of dinner until the black thread to sew up the turkey is found."

Now heaven knows where the black thread hid itself but though we searched everywhere it didn't turn up. I emptied my make-up bag, Jennifer her piggy-bank, and I discovered Daisy poking among the ashes of the dining room fire. Laura says she searched under every bed. I doubt it. She was probably up stairs having a snooze on one of the beds.

On the principle of the thing, mummy insisted that each of us contribute a pound towards the thread. Laura said she had never heard anything so ridiculous and refused to pay up. So she was refused dinner.

She wasn't missing much. It was Irish stew, vegetarian style. She sat at the table drinking tea until mummy saw her and demanded to know why she wasn't eating anything.

"There will be no anorexics in my house," she stormed. As there was no stew left over in the pot we each had to give her a spoonful of ours.

"You might starve yourself in Dublin," she said,

"But you will eat properly when you are at home."

I think she was satisfied then that she had wreaked enough havoc, because she settled down and behaved afterwards.

No sooner had she shut up than daddy began. His menopause manifested itself in an intensified interest in religion. Jennifer says it was because he was elected on to the church committee: it went to his head. I never minded Rev Robinson's sermons, though he never gave us as much Hell and Damnation as some ministers. I found daddy's interpretation and reiteration hard to swallow with the stew.

Later in the afternoon he offered to make the stuffing to save mummy's wrist. I suspect he felt guilty about not cutting the sticks himself. It was only after he had finished that mummy let it slip that she had bought the bread a week ago. Suddenly daddy could smell blue mould off the stuffing.

"Don't be so stupid," said mummy. "You smell parsley."

"The man is the head of the woman," daddy orated majestically. "I am the head of this household and if I say that the stuffing smells of blue mould then the stuffing smells of blue mould."

Laura and I were listening and she mouthed at me, "His head is cut, we have mental parents. Jennifer isn't sixteen yet, she'll have to be taken into care."

Daddy jammed the bowl under my nose.

"Sniff that," he commanded, "tell me if it smells of blue mould."

I don't know if blue mould has a smell, I doubt it.

"I smell onions and parsley," I said, and left for a two-hour walk in the hope that all would be calm on my return.

It wasn't of course.

Everyone was getting ready for the Sunday evening carol service. Having spent the earlier part of the Sabbath quoting Holy Scripture and the minister, daddy was effing and blinding magnificently because he couldn't find the hairspray. Mummy was bathing her wrist and complaining that the doctor hadn't stitched her arm properly.

Jennifer was playing a solo on the flute at the carol service. "Silent Night" started strong and clear but after the high note at the end of the fifth line, she seemed to choke and suddenly no noise came out. Where had the last line gone?

Obviously Jennifer wasn't waiting to find out and she snapped her music from the font and dashed back into the choir. Sarah was also in the choir and she wore such a grave expression that Laura and I almost laughed out loud. Daddy's look—which would have soured milk—stopped us.

Daisy, who hadn't realised that there was another

line in "Silent Night" whispered, "What's so funny? I thought she played beautifully."

Because no one really grew up at Derryrose, Christmas morning held the same excitement as when we were children. Laura crept into my bedroom about half past six and into my bed, only to discover Henry cuddled up beside me.

"Helen," she hissed maniacally, "Helen, let go that dog and come on—Santa's been." She had been waking me up with "Santa's been" on Christmas morning since I had been five years old.

Daisy (17), Sarah (16), and Jennifer (15) were waiting on the hall landing, chattering with cold. Jennifer, a mite sarcastic by nature, whispered, "I suppose if the fire was left on Santa couldn't get down the chimney."

"Nonsense," Daisy cut in, "you know he has a magic key."

I had the same gut feeling of excitement now as when I was a child, as we crept down the creaking staircase to the dining room.

Laura stopped with her hand on the doorknob. Dramatic as always.

"Do you think he has gone?"

Once when she had been a very small child she had caught Santa Claus in the dining room. She had been cautious ever since.

"Cut the crap, my feet are freezing." Jennifer had no soul.

The door eased open and we tiptoed into the big room, sighing voluptuously in unison as we did every year. Then we fell on our presents.

"That blasted silage stinks," said Jennifer, rapidly draining the glass of sherry we had left out for Santa, before anyone could stop her. "The reindeer never eat it, Daisy. I can't think why you don't try them with hay or molasses, or something more tasty."

Daisy was oblivious to the complaints of Jennifer. Already she was picking out Chopin's Waltz in C Sharp Major on the piano. I had a feeling that we would be ready to crucify Santa and Daisy and Chopin by the end of this day of goodwill to all pianists.

Santa had left me a scarlet evening-dress, so obvious and so blasé that I was shy touching it. It resembled the dress Scarlett O'Hara wore to Ashley's surprise birthday party. I could imagine mummy sewing it and watching *Gone with the Wind* on the video machine. The dress more than compensated for the massive belly-warming bloomers, the thermal vest and the ankle-length heavy-duty nightdress also left for me.

When mummy and daddy joined us—about seven o'clock—I kissed her enthusiastically.

"The dress is a dream," I said.

"Go up and give gran-gran a kiss," she said. "She did all the hard bits."

Gran-gran, daddy's mother, lived with us in Derryrose. She and mummy had hated each other at first when mummy and daddy had married—power struggle. Years together and we children had mellowed both of them and they had even been known to speak to each other.

"The Mistress of Derryrose," as she called herself, rarely bothered anybody now. She lived in the past most of the time and called me Maisie a lot. Great-aunt Maisie was her sister and they hadn't spoken to each other in over half a century. I was told I resembled Maisie which was somewhat disconcerting as Maisie was a nutcase and lived in Donegal. Whenever we visited her she would play classical music on her gramophone and smoke long cigarettes through a pipe, and she drank like a fish. If I really thought I was like her I would drown myself.

Daddy, of course, had managed to choose the worst present possible for mummy—a galvanised steel bucket.

"Well," said mummy, "what's this for?"

"Why for taking the ashes out of the fire," he said, not even looking at her. He was screwing up the courage to thank Daisy for the dreadful tie she had chosen for him—no one could accuse daddy of being romantic.

"You must wear my tie to church this morning," Daisy insisted, forgetting for one brief moment her Chopin. We always wore our Christmas presents to church on Christmas morning. In a lot of cases that was the only time we wore them.

But it was Richard's present that gave me greatest pleasure. *Emily's Quest* is only a child's book but I had read it so many times that I knew the chapters by heart. Yet I had never seen it in shops, only on library shelves.

"Only you know why you love it," he had written on the inside cover. He had signed himself Richard JF Knight which made me laugh because it was as if we didn't know each other. Richard JF Knight was emotionally barren.

While I dressed for church Laura showed me Mick's present. A G-string looks like the most uncomfortable thing in the world, and I'm not surprised that the label on the packet said, "Worn with pride, removed with pleasure."

"Isn't it cool?" said Laura parading in front of the mirror, admiring her reflection. Gloomily I compared the string with the balloon-sized bloomers I was swaddled in.

"You'll catch a chill," I suggested, more than a little envious.

"Yeah," she laughed, "But what a way to go. Imagine if we are in a car accident on the way to church and men have to undress us?"

"I'd rather not," I answered primly, thinking of the laugh they'd get seeing my bloomers.

"I see Anto the Onion sent you writing-paper again this year." Laura was smothering herself in the strawberry talcum powder Sarah had given me.

"Mmm," I had cheered up somewhat now the bloomers were concealed by the tweed mini-skirt Laura had bought me.

"And he used a page of it to tell me that he hoped to see me at church this morning but if I wasn't there he would phone and arrange something about the Boxing Night dance."

"Oh Helen," Laura screwed up her nose. "Why can't he leave you alone? He's an absolute plonker."

Anto and I had gone to school together and at a school dance when we were sixteen he had said:

"Helen, if I wasn't a gentleman I would take you into a corner."

I think I had said something like: "Oh Anthony, if I wasn't a lady I would go with you," but I hadn't meant it, of course, because everybody, even harmless tarts like me, has to draw the line somewhere.

My cousins joined us in the gallery of the 1st Presbyterian church. Aunt Louise carried Ernest who was four months old and who was sick over her during the service. Henry, five and hyperactive, spent the entire service dropping Jelly Tots on to the heads of the congregation beneath him, and when he had exhausted his supply of Jelly Tots he dropped his hymn book instead. Fortunately there were no casualties.

"That child is lost for a good spanking," said grangran, who had forgotten that Henry was her grandson. I enjoyed the Christmas morning service when the kids brought up their presents to show Rev Robinson. We had a job restraining Daisy who was convinced that the Rev wanted to see her sheet music. I didn't really think the Rev would appreciate my evening dress and Laura's G-string.

I gave Anto the Onion the slip at the church door but he came pounding after me to the carpark and cornered me, his face wreathed in smiles.

"Helen darling! I thought I had missed you."

"Anthony, darling." I thought I had missed him too.

Anto the Onion talked for a while and I smiled and fluttered my eyelashes at him automatically and Laura revved up the Morris. Jennifer, who had no manners, stuck her head out the window and yelled, "Come on Helen, stop flirting with Anto, I'm dying to go to the loo."

I think he finalised arrangements about the Boxing Day dance but I can't guarantee it. I wasn't really listening.

Gran-gran treated us all to a glass of her QC sherry before dinner. Mummy had sent Sarah into the off-licence a week before to buy VC sherry by mistake. Poor Sarah, who once claimed to feel incongruous when her earrings were upside down, had been mortified when she discovered the mistake.

We drank a couple of bottles of gran-gran's gooseberry wine too with the turkey and my head was a little light afterwards.

"I see Dublin hasn't improved your table manners," daddy said when I wiped my nose with the cuff of my cardigan.

After dinner with traditional diligence we ate our way through our selection boxes—Jennifer won, she ate 3 bars of chocolate during the Queen's speech—and I fed so much turkey to Henry he went to sleep behind the piano. Then gran-gran sang "Oh Come All You Faithful"—the effects of more than QC sherry methinks—and asked Maisie—me—to accompany her in "Once In Royal David's City."

I suspect daddy was imbibing the same stuff as gran-gran because he loosened the tie Daisy had forced him into and spun mummy into a wild flurry of barndancing—jiving—quick-stepping to an Irish music tape Laura had stolen from Mick. They spun round the kitchen until my head was light and they were so exhausted that they had to go and lie down together.

We girls had a more dignified waltzing session. Jennifer swept gran-gran into a turn which made her so dizzy we thought we had killed her. I thought of Anto running after me after church and Richard's formal signature on the inside cover of my book. I wondered if Richard wore a paper hat or if his parents danced in the kitchen. Somehow I didn't think so.

"You've lost a lot of spots," Patterson Hamilton said to me. He had lost his National Health spectacles and any sense he ever had. Puffing with concentrated enthusiasm at a cigarette and manhandling a pint of Guinness he turned to Laura beside me, voluptuous in her clinging black Lycra, and commented luxuriously:

"And you have gained a few things, Laura."

Laura and I glanced at each other and dissolved into unsophisticated giggles. It was madness of course for us to tart ourselves up. Magherafelt couldn't really handle two Gordons, what with Laura hanging out of her black dress and me flaunting my little red number.

"We'll show them," we had decided in my firelit bedroom.

"Whorish dresses," mummy had said, half admiring, half disapproving. She had hurried us out before daddy caught sight of us or doubtless he would have sent us straight back upstairs to change into frilly blouses and knee-length skirts.

I encountered Anto the Onion with the Soft-Boiled Eyes to give him his unabridged title at the door of the Rugby Club. Surely it wasn't the same glass of fizzy orange as last year?

"What sort of get-up do you call that?" he questioned me when I took my jacket off. His eyes were protruding on stalks.

"Did no one ever teach you to talk to girls, Anthony?" It was Hugh Stewart, whom I had had a crush on at school.

"I recognised the potential in those legs when you were fourteen," said Hugh, unashamedly admiring them. "I told you I would marry a woman with legs like yours; do you remember me saying that?"

Of course I remembered, I had lain awake all night and thought about it five years ago. But he had been two years above me at school and I had been shy at fourteen and by the time I had blossomed at sixteen he had left for university in a blaze of academic glory. Anto wanted to dance with me and Patter was demanding a dance from Laura. It was the season of goodwill so we took to the floor with them. The music was really boppy and I shook my stuff as they say.

"Are you drunk?" Anto looked scandalised by my exhibition. He danced as if he was a puppet and there was no one around to move the strings.

"I am not." I was rather offended.

It was just typical that a slow set of dances started at that moment, and Anto grabbed at me the way you grab a half hundredweight bag of potatoes, before you yank them onto your shoulder.

Anto said, "You know, Helen, I fell for you first time I saw you." As he was really sober I think he meant it. Or rather I think he thought he meant it. I didn't laugh as I was overcome with pity for anyone who loved me when I loved only myself. Easy come, easy go.

Anto was a very suitable young man, he was training to be a doctor, but he had the sex appeal of a potato with blight. After all, he wore a vest.

Laura suddenly descended on me and propelled me into the ladies loo. Slashing on her lipstick she commented: "Looks as if five years of metamorphosis mean nothing to the likes of Patterson and Anto. When I suggested to Patterson that we dance over to yourself and Anto the Onion he said, 'Oh no, leave them alone, they belong together.' I had to take action so I told Patterson that we had promised mummy that we would be home at midnight, as the roads are slippy, and it was time for us to leave."

She smirked. "And of course Patterson believed it and said something like, 'Oh yes, your mother always insists that you are home early on big nights. Anthony says you are a very respectable family, and that Helen would make a very respectable wife.' I think you should thank me: Anto the Onion was on the verge of proposal there."

We hid in the loos until we were sure that Anthony and Patterson had left, then re-emerged. I was swept off by Hugh Stewart and Laura by Willie Johnston, who was a fine thing by anybody's reckoning. I had always wanted to shift Hugh and could hardly believe my luck that he had thrown himself at me so conveniently. Not a very ladylike way of looking at it but I was nineteen, pretty and wild, and in search of a bit of excitement. I think Hugh understood. He was a very good shift. I wasn't disappointed that he didn't ask to see me again because he was so fanciable it would have broken my heart to refuse him. But of course I couldn't go out with him again. I had my reputation to consider. Helen Gordon never shifted the same man more than once, point of honour, no matter who he was. I did think of Anto the Onion once as I left the Rugby Club, and a tiny twinge of conscience hit me. But I couldn't help it if I didn't want him.

CHAPTER FOUR

After the excitement of Christmas at Derryrose I found UCD very dull and squandered a lot of my grant money taking the bus home at weekends. Laura was delighted and encouraged me to make these trips as it meant that she could have Mighty Mick to stay in our room in the hostel. How she got Mick smuggled past the warden I never tried to discover.

Mummy fretted that I was becoming introverted travelling home all the time, and I hadn't the heart to tell her that Thursday night was the big night out for Ag students, the weekend I required for recuperation. So when she encouraged me to take Daisy and Sarah dancing to the nightclubs in Portrush I had to refuse.

"Helen darling," she said, "I think there is something the matter with Daisy: she doesn't appear to be interested in men."

"You mean, she prefers women?" I was surprised. Daisy had never struck me as a lesbian.

"No, of course not," said mummy, shocked. Homosexuality shocked my mother, frightened my father.

"But she is eighteen almost, Helen, and she has never had a boyfriend. I mean, you have had little boys walking out from Magherafelt to see you for years."

I had to smile—I sounded like Catherine the Great, or Mata Hari, or Cleopatra.

"Daisy is a bit vague," I suggested kindly. "I don't think she notices men, so I suppose they don't notice her."

"Yes dear," said mummy, "precisely."

"And I suppose she frightens them a bit," I added, "because they feel she doesn't need them. And men like to feel needed."

"But can't you help her, Helen?"

Help her? As far as I could see Daisy was beyond help, but of course I didn't tell mummy that. So instead I suggested that she pass her A Levels, then come to Dublin and live with Laura and me, and we would sort her out.

It appeared however that Daisy hadn't a clue what she wanted to study.

"I thought over Christmas that I would like to study French," she confided in me one Sunday afternoon in February, when we were walking the meadows with Henry and Brenda. "The language is so beautiful but the French are such a volatile race, they frighten me, and I loathe garlic in food. And then I thought English because literature is life, isn't it?" I disagreed with her of course, literature to me was escapism, but it's a well-known fact that it is both foolish and dangerous to argue with mad sisters.

"Daisy," I said gently, "You are studying science."

She shook her head, and for the first time I noticed how outrageous her blue velvet beret looked on the top of her fair head.

"I know," she said sadly. "I was inappropriately advised. So I am going to Dublin to study Ag Science with you, dear."

She grabbed my arm with a surprising firm grip.

"But what worries me, Helen: are all the girls pretty in Dublin city as they are in the song? Will I be of inferior calibre in comparison?"

Sarah had caught herself a boyfriend by the time Laura and I came home for our Easter holidays. Mummy cried when she told us because she considered Daisy to be on the shelf and destined to a life of spinsterhood.

"But I don't see the connection," said Laura afterwards, "Just because Sarah is younger than Daisy. And she is so boringly beautiful too. If we were all blind, she would have nothing going for her."

It appeared that Ian, for that was the young man's name, visited the house, and actually came into the sitting room to talk to mummy when he waited for Sarah. Any young man who visited our house more than once was either a fool or very keen. Ian, we suspected, was both. Mummy always lay in wait for the young men, nabbed them at the front door and imprisoned them in the sitting room to find out if their intentions were honourable. If she approved of him we knew he was going to be a bore. She approved of Ian. I had never kept a boyfriend long enough for her to check him out.

Daddy refused to have anything to do with the "boyfriend" and hid in the outside loo when he appeared. If he answered the telephone and it was Ian he always said, "Wrong number," and slammed down the receiver. I think he was shy.

Sarah, who was only sixteen, and much too young for boyfriends, had met Ian at a church party when he had picked her as his wife in "The Farmer Wants a Wife." They had sat together during the religious chat that marked time out at these dos and shared a bottle of lemonade blowing through the straw to make bubbles. Then he had left her home in his Toyota Corolla Twin Cam. He spoke of the car with the reverence Mick reserved for Laura's big breasts.

Laura and I interrogated in our own way. He didn't laugh at Laura's favourite joke: "Does a rooster have a penis? No it has a cock." and he failed the dress test by wearing a pink shirt. However, his eyes lit up behind his DUP spectacles when Sarah appeared, and his family was very rich. He was studying accountancy himself. This elevated him immeasurably in both mummy and Sarah's eyes. I think he was afraid of Laura who told him she believed in sex before marriage as impotency was rife in men who wore too-tight jeans. I felt a bit sorry for him because he had sweaty palms and he hoovered out the Twin Cam every Friday night before he came courting. In fact, in fairness even, Ian imitated manhood quite well. He spoke beautifully—elocution lessons we guessed—and his fingernails were always clean and never chewed. He never kept Sarah out later than her deadline and he was never late for a date. We suspected that he hid at the bottom of the drive watching the clock so that he would arrive at 8pm on the dot. Mummy worshipped him for his punctuality because daddy had never been early in his life. Even on her wedding-day, when it's a bride's prerogative to be late, he had kept mummy standing at the altar for over an hour—he had been calving a cow. It must have been rather funny, mummy sweeping up the church on her father's arm to find no bridegroom at the other end.

Derryrose is terribly beautiful in the spring. Grangran was a devoted gardener and the orchards and the lawns around the old house were alive with the flowers of spring. Snowdrops, dew-pearled peeping out of the damp grass, daffodils in the breeze, borders of tulips and crocus flaming colour. She often joined me in the afternoons to sit on the stone pew in the orchard and drink in the silence.

"Maisie," she said one quiet sunlit day when young clouds raced each other overhead, "Maisie, I am sorry about Kenneth. It was my fault he married me and not you. I never loved him, you know, not the way you did, and I could never handle him the way you could. And you were such a sweet sister, such fun we had together until Kenneth came back from South Africa and married me not you."

Gran-gran was a little dotty we knew, because she was old, and I patted her tiny hand.

"I know," I said. "I know."

I found her slumped in an undignified heap beside her bed the next morning, her hand still clutching the tweed skirt she had been buttoning. She looked very small dead and I lifted her easily on to the bed, and sat down beside her. There was no need to rush to phone the coroner and undertaker—death is timeless. I didn't feel sad. Gran-gran had been waiting to die for years. So I patted her hand a bit and kissed the clay and went down stairs.

The ensuing hysteria and tears gave me a headache and I escaped into Magherafelt to get ham and bread for the wake. Jennifer, who was her pet, cried until her face swole and she looked hideous, and mummy, who had never liked gran-gran, cried so much that she had to wear sunglasses though it was March and raining. Henry my terrier howled and howled but that was because we all forgot to feed him, not because he grieved for gran-gran who kicked him once when he got under her feet.

Wakes are great social gatherings round our country. It gives the men a chance to discuss the Orange lodge and the women an opportunity to bitch about each other in undertones befitting the gloom.

Aunt Sarah, gran-gran's only daughter, arrived on the second day in floods of tears and it didn't seem the occasion to remind her that she hadn't visited her mother since Christmas. I restrained such uncharitable thoughts and left my mother to voice them instead, to her sister while they buttered the twelfth loaf of ham sandwiches. I dreamed one night that I was being chased by a giant ham sandwich.

The orchard seemed more silent those two days of gran-gran's wake. I spent a lot of time there. When it was wet I lay in the hayloft reading. Anywhere rather than be exposed to the claustrophobic funeral atmosphere shrouding Derryrose.

On the day of the funeral Sarah met me leaving the sitting room with the vacuum cleaner.

"You didn't clean round her?"

"Sure did." I felt flippant. "And she never said a word."

Sarah went a paler shade of green and mentioned something about throwing up. Ian was her rock and comforter through this traumatic time; he hardly left Derryrose and we fed him so many ham sandwiches he started looking like a pig. I think he thought he had got his feet firmly under the table.

"Does he have no home to go to?" I asked Sarah who said I had no manners.

The funeral service was a nightmare because it poured and poured.

"Oh I wish the sun could have shone," wailed Aunt Sarah. So did I, my navy shoes were ruined.

Great-aunt Maisie drove herself down from Donegal that morning. She was wearing well when you considered she lived alone and had so many bad habits. She had a great head of black hair that we always admired when we visited her, but the blackberries that she used to dye it mustn't have been ripe enough as there was a purple sheen off it on the day of the funeral. She swept into the church and informed Rev Robinson that as chief mourner she was going to read the lesson. It was the most obscure piece of Scripture I have ever heard, I think she read the wrong piece by accident. She got a bit carried away being in the pulpit and led us in prayer as well.

Daddy said afterwards that that was what happened when you educated women—Aunt Maisie was one of the first women to go to Queen's University in Belfast. She had gone there after gran-gran had married Kenneth. Listening to Aunt Maisie in the pulpit I reckoned he had had a lucky escape. There was tea and ham sandwiches after the service for the mourners, and I felt the need to talk to Aunt Maisie. I wanted her to know that gran-gran was sorry she had married Kenneth. I explained haltingly to my great-aunt, who was even more terrifying in the flesh than she was in the pulpit. It sounded so silly, repeating the senile ramblings of a dotty old lady but Aunt Maisie didn't laugh. She held my hand in the same vice-grip that Daisy had and said, "Thank you dear, it's good for me to know that the dead can now rest."

Only after the last mourner left did Derryrose breathe again.

The afternoon of the funeral our pony Romeo escaped into the meadows and gorged himself on new grass and had foundered feet before any of us realised that he had got away. Santa Claus had brought us Romeo when I was ten and over the years he had bucked us repeatedly into hawthorn bushes, bit us with abandon and stopped dead at almost every jump we had put him at. He had never been easy to catch, always spinning his heels to us at the last minute just when you thought you had him, and the fact that he let us halter him immediately indicated that he was fairly sick. He was in so much pain that Jennifer, who was with me, had to crack a stick with bailer twine attached to it just behind his rump to get him to move at all. All three of us were soaked by the time we got from the meadows to the farmyard.

Romeo was closed into an empty cubicle house without food in the hope that the laminitis was only a mild attack. He sulked terribly and wouldn't look at any of us, gazing mournfully over the gate at the green grass that had poisoned him.

We all visited him at intervals through the day but he lost the will to live, lay down and refused to get up.

Jennifer shouted and Daisy cried and Laura lay on the ground with her head beside his and tried to talk him through it step by step—horse psychology, she said. He pretended not to hear her, so daddy, with sadistic efficiency, whacked him across the rump until he staggered to his feet. If there were vultures in Ireland I think they would have been circling the cubicle house.

Ian couldn't grasp the dimensions of this catastrophe though Sarah took him out to visit Romeo. He said he thought Romeo was a pretty colour.

"Palamino," Jennifer snapped.

She rode best of us all and had been known to jump him over the ironing board on one of his better days. She had taken him to a gymkhana once and he had won "The Pony with the Biggest Eyes" and "The "Pony with the Longest Tail" but he had refused the first jump three times in the jumping ring, had thrown Jennifer and ambled off to eat the second jump. Then Sarah got a flea.

Mummy blamed Romeo, Sarah blamed Henry and we blamed Ian who was too clean to be wholesome. She was allergic to insect bites and swole up alarmingly. Rather than let Ian see her short of perfect she left instructions that she didn't want to speak to him should he telephone. He always telephoned her on a Thursday night. Daisy took the phone call and said

"Oh Ian, I'm sorry but Sarah says she doesn't want to talk to you."

When Sarah heard what Daisy had said she retired to bed to scratch her insect bites and cry, convinced that her life was over.

Ian, however, assumed that she was studying. He was such an awful bore. My legs would go to sleep when I was with him.

Romeo had gone to the glue factory by the time Laura and I got home from college in June. Diligently we had inquired after him every week when we phoned home, and every week mummy muttered something about there being no improvement. It seems he had been put out of his misery the week our exams had started and mummy was convinced the grief would kill Laura if she found out. As I hadn't cried for gran-gran there was little chance I would cry for Romeo.

I was afraid that it was going to be a long summer without Romeo and gran-gran and was delighted when daddy got me a job milking cows for a friend of his who had gone for a fortnight's holiday over the Twelfth. None of us had ever heard of a farmer taking holidays before. Johnny Paisley—Ruth Paisley's ex—lent me his Mini to drive to and from the farm and Jennifer came with me "for the experience." I'm not sure if she wanted experience of getting up early in the morning or milking cows but she was fairly useless in the parlour, whatever the reason.

On the first morning she wailed, "Helen there is no vacuum in the thingy; I can't get it to stick to her udder."

It turned out that she had been trying to put the clusters on the cow upside down. I think some people are lucky with cows and some aren't: Jennifer was always in the wrong place at the wrong time and was urinated on and kicked constantly. We got stopped one morning by a police patrol.

"Do you realise you are speeding?" one officer said.

The Mini, which was a bit of a crock, stalled on me and Jennifer, rude as always, piped up and said, "We are milkmaids, and we are late for work."

There was no tax on the Mini and it was not insured, and it refused to start. The policemen who were going off duty had to tow us the rest of the way to Paisley's; they suggested we find alternative transport. I enjoyed milking cows though it got monotonous after a while. Sarah preached at me on the immorality of accepting Income Support along with my pay but I figured that I required compensation for rising at five in the morning and enduring Jennifer's incompetence. The Mini died for good a couple of days before Johnny was due back from Scotland—he had been at a pipe band competition—and I had to substitute his tractor for the Mini. I shouldn't have minded if the tractor had been a flashy model with air conditioning and a stereo but the Massey had no doors, no windows and no brakes for that matter.

Determined not to be outdone on the workfront Laura decided to get an illegal job too. She had spent the first month home lying round the house and getting under everyone's feet. Once I recorded her movements for an entire day:

12.15pm: rose, showered, looked at herself.

1pm: breakfast, watched *Neighbours* on the television, scratched, dressed, read Jackie Collins novel.

3pm: ate fry, watched Children's television.

5pm: watched potatoes boil dry. Read the *Sun* as milk for the custard boiled over.

6pm: ate tea then watched television until 12 midnight.

She started washing dishes at a restaurant near home. She complained that it was a backbreaking and thankless task and her nails flaked in the hot water. Then she had a row with one of the waitresses at the end of the first month because Laura claimed that the waitress had stolen her doggy bag, and was sacked for screaming "thieving bitch" and throwing a milk jug at her. The row was overheard by a wedding-party in the dining room and there had been turkey and ham in the doggy bag, for Henry and Brenda. Laura was delighted to give up the manual labour of course but she said that she felt as if she had failed the dogs.

So she got herself work in a chip-van next. It was mighty crack, she said, rattling round the countryside chatting to the natives but that spell lasted only briefly too. Edith the woman who owned the van complained that she gave too generous helpings of chips, undercooked the sausages, couldn't count in her head and always gave back the correct change.

"How can I make a profit," she said, "if you are going to be so honest?"

She sacked her when Laura suggested that she was so fat she must be eating any profit.

"The honest business was a bit of a joke really," Laura explained afterwards while we were cutting the lawn. "I was carrying home sausages and burgers for Henry and Brenda constantly."

Her only sadness was that she couldn't afford to visit Mick in London, where he was working on a building site.

"I'll never find a pair of hands as large here," she moaned.

CHAPTER FIVE

D aisy did in fact join Laura and me in Dublin the
next year to study agricultural science and we
took a basement flat in Palmerston Road.

With only Sarah and Jennifer at home mummy
and daddy got "empty-nest syndrome" and bought a
flock of sheep to amuse themselves. Daddy got very
excited at the thought of the lambing and drew up a
rota to include all of us getting up to check them in
the middle of the night.

Daisy's arrival in the Ag block caused a sensation.
Whereas I was labelled a "harmless tart" she was
denounced as "mental" and "eccentric" by students
and lecturers alike. If she wasn't getting totally
confused by her timetable and attending the wrong
lecture she was to be seen knitting in the back row.

"Hellish," she said one day after a maths lecture.
"I got the entire pattern wrong because I was
concentrating on the differentiation and not on the
rib. I was so engrossed that I knit the waistband a
foot long."

"Is she really your sister?" my classmates asked. I

was surprised by their surprise because there is a striking family resemblance between all my sisters and there aren't many northern accents in the Ag block.

Mick explained, "You are such a tart, Helen, in that mini-skirt and lipstick and your hair all over your face. Daisy, bless her, hasn't a streetwise brain in her head. She looks like Anne of Green Gables and you act like Scarlett O'Hara."

I, of course, was more than a little flattered to be compared to my idol but Daisy's supposed role-model concerned me somewhat. I didn't like the idea of the world considering her eccentric even if I did. Privately Laura and I felt that if she ever once discovered men our problems would be history.

"But Helen..." Daisy reasoned when I suggested as much to her. "But Helen, men never seem to interfere with me the way they do with you. Mummy has suggested a number of times that I am now old enough to have a boyfriend but just because I have been given permission doesn't mean that a young man automatically materialises."

Things came to a head when Laura and I decided to have a Christmas dinner party in the flat after our exams. It mattered not that only one ring worked on the cooker and that we owned only one saucepan, the one that I boiled my underwear in on Saturday mornings. Daisy then made homemade soup in it on Saturday afternoon to feed us through the week. She once made the soup without washing out the saucepan first and there was a crust of Lux flakes around the edge. The soup tasted grand.

We had been reared on the principle of "Why spend money on food when you can spend it on clothes!"—quote unquote, mummy—and we modified it to suit ourselves.

It goes without saying that Laura spent her money having a good time, and my grant cheque went to the Second Hand Bookshop in Rathmines. God only knows what Daisy spent her money on. I suspect that she left most of it sitting round and forgot about it. She steeped jeans once with a ten-pound note in the pocket and dried the money and her jeans on the line side by side.

Each of us was to invite one male guest to the party. This guest would be required to bring a bottle of wine and to behave like a gentleman. The first we believed most men capable of, the second would be touch and go. Mick said he was bringing cider, because only yuppies drank wine and cider got you drunk faster. Laura said that she knew he was a bogtrotter but she never realised that he was an embarrassment as well. Mick was refused all carnal courting pleasures and, denied the nookie, he came round pretty fast.

Daisy had major problems concerning the date issue for the dinner party. She couldn't remember the names of half the men in her class. "They are all Mick or John," she protested. "And they all look exactly the same."

She threatened to ask the girl who did her chemistry practicals with her rather than approach a member of the opposite sex.

"It's not that I don't like them or that I'm afraid of them but I think they are afraid of me," which actually didn't surprise me since she had bullied all of them into forfeiting their beer money in a collection for "Save the Rain-forests."

But she was shockingly unGordonlike in her man-catching inadequacy. Unrepentantly man-mad I couldn't fathom her. Here was a healthy heterosexual maiden, dammit, a Gordon, threatening to invite a woman to our dinner party. I choked at the thought, and admonished her to reconsider. The poor girl was overwhelmed by my persuasive petitions and an expression of panic began flitting across her face every time she encountered me.

Changing tactics I then suggested that perhaps it was up to her to go and find herself a suitor—as I found them for myself time and time again.

"Oh I couldn't," eyes wide with wonder, "How unmaidenly! How fast!"

"Oh Daisy," I grumbled, "Daisy, do you think Jane Eyre caught Mr Rochester by hiding in the nursery with that child she was governess to? No, she was giving him the 'come-on' from the start; and as for Elizabeth Bennet in *Pride and Prejudice*, she was flirting with Darcy. 'Chase me, chase me!' And if it comes to the bit," I added feeling decidedly fast, "I guarantee that Mary often winked at Joseph in the Bible."

"I can't," said Daisy pathetically, but she could, and she did, and my pious Presbyterian prayers were answered.

Standing in the foodhall in Dunnes Stores unable to decide whether to buy Branflakes or Alpen a mystery voice behind her said, "Buy the Alpen; it's on Special Offer this week."

Bullseyed by Cupid's arrow Daisy—when she told us later—said that violins began to play as their eyes met.

"And I simply asked him to the dinner party," she said. "It was you speaking through me, Helen, because you both know how retarded I am with men."

Laura nodded rather insensitively but I made a face at her in case she said anything.

"Do you think it was very forward of me?"—anxiously—"Sharing a bedroom with you is making me loose, Helen."

I patted her hand encouragingly as anyone could

see the excitement had exhausted most of her stamina. Vaguely I tried to recall the days when I was in the first flush of such emotion, probably from afar, with Hugh Stewart but I had never been afflicted with love throughout my man-eating career, and there was a world of difference between them. I almost envied her the turbulence she appeared to be feeling over the Muesli prince—Daisy, true to form, had forgotten to ask him his name.

"It just never occurred to me," she said, "But don't worry, I will be able to recognise him again."

Laura thought the whole thing was hysterical.

"I'm sending up prayers constantly to thank God that she is your faculty and not my own," she told me. "If it's a sales rep for Alpen that she has picked up, do you think he will give us free samples?"

If it was possible, Daisy was in even more of a dither than usual the afternoon of our dinner party. I returned home from a woeful geology exam, heavy laden with parcels of food for the dinner, to find her head bobbing above a sea of papers and notes and aimless manuscripts on our bedroom floor.

Enquiring I discovered that she was tidying. Further questioning as to what precisely she was tidying and her abstract head became panic-stricken.

"Oh Helen, I appreciate that it is a bit untidy but why tidy somewhere that is not untidy." I thought immediately of the living room—"pigsty" leapt to mind.

"That cupboard..." she continued, "that cupboard has been crying out for organisation. I have found all the lists I've made since October and thought I had forgotten." She presented me with a piece of bailer twine.

"Daisy,"—she was probably disturbed but we had no tranquillisers and no strait-jacket in the flat and she certainly wasn't getting the port I had saved for after dinner—"Daisy, come into the kitchen, you are overwrought." I led her from the havoc, and once I had established her washing potatoes I reinstated the cupboard contents back in their rightful place—back in chaos in the cupboard.

Her shopping list from October I glanced at with amusement. "Elastic to hold up pyjamas"—well she had never got round to buying pyjamas elastic: they were still safely pinned. Sultana Bran was starred. None of us liked Sultana Bran but there was a Free Gift Offer at the time for spring bulbs—and Daisy planned to give them to me for Christmas. I recalled picking seventy-five sultanas out of my plate one morning.

While I baked an apple tart—pudding for the party—I scrutinised Daisy objectively. Fat, fair pigtails and a Paisley print pinafore—Ulster's answer to Anne of Green Gables. Mick was right. I had never met the Muesli prince but I knew that no man, however avantgarde his taste, was going to find that pinafore sexy. And my speciality was sexuality, not apple tart, so I knew.

Tactfully I offered her my favourite skirt, first cousin to a mini-skirt, that finished just above the knee. She had such good legs it was a shame to hide them beneath acres of Paisley print.

"Your mini-skirt? But I never wear mini-skirts. I would feel very wicked exposing that much flesh."

"You won't be exposing anything," I persuaded her. "You can wear stockings and cover up all the flesh."

The dreamy eyes remained doubtful, like a slightly bewildered pussy-cat, I thought. I noticed cigarette ash on the table after I had the pastry rolled out. Daisy hadn't noticed—too busy thinking beautiful thoughts of the Muesli prince—so I finished the tart and stuck it in the oven. Wiping the table I played my trump card.

"Even Richard approves of the skirt, D, and you know what a strait-laced Victorian he is."

"But Richard approves of everything you wear," she smiled. "He dotes on you."

Daisy was very fond of Richard, whom she classed as a kindred spirit, a man who could distinguish between a waltz and a symphony, and who often accompanied us to the National Concert Hall for recitals.

I smiled too. "Except my black jeans with the zips, my short mini-skirt, my tie-dyed shirt, my black party dress and my purple tights—he loathes the purple tights with a passion." The list was endless, the list of things Richard disapproved of. Of course he never said anything but he snorted terribly when I wore them.

And then half an hour before the guests were due to arrive, disaster struck. The doorbell buzzed, and Daisy—thinking it was the Muesli prince—bolted into the bathroom and bolted the door in the agony of first-love embarrassment.

Three-quarters made up, and inwardly cursing Laura, who had disappeared about lunch time to buy crackers, I wrenched open the front door.

A rabbit person from home called Sandra Jackson stood on the door step. She had been in Laura's class at school and had gone to Rev Robinson's church. I think she was studying something at Trinity College. When we had met her at church over the summer Laura and I had always effusively invited her to visit us in Dublin. Neither of us liked her but that wasn't the point, neither of us had ever thought she would take us up on the offer. And today of all days, with our dinner party, and the Muesli prince and all that wine we were expecting, today the prim little rabbit had decided to visit.

"Sandra," I said, "what a surprise." She was wearing a duffel coat, and I had to invite her in. She was sitting on our best armchair, her eyes scrutinising the living room, drinking our coffee and criticising the dampness of basement flats when I heard Laura thumping through the front door accompanied by Mick's booming laughter. Daisy's expression of mesmerised good manners became one of panic and our eyes met above Sandra's page-boy haircut. How were we going to get rid of the rabbit before she encountered Mick and Laura? I could imagine Sandra racing from our flat to the nearest telephone to spread the glad tidings: the Gordon girls are loose women entertaining drunken Catholics and we thought them all such decent girls—and Sarah a Sunday school teacher too! I was terrified, Daisy looked as if she were about to go into a swoon.

"We are having dinner with a couple of friends, Sandra," I said loudly, clutching at straws, wildly hoping Laura would cop on and conceal Mighty Mick in the bedroom until Sandra could be removed.

"Oh," said the rabbit, "that's nice," and she continued drinking our coffee and conducting her monologue about the nicer class of people studying at Trinity College.

"You are such a rabbit," I thought viciously smiling outwardly and pulling my already low shirt lower for badness. "You horrid Magherafelt rabbit, persecuting us and ruining our dinner party, noseying into our lives when you know damn well we can't stick you."

"You'll have to excuse me a minute," said Daisy suddenly, grey with fright, and she dashed from the living room. Out of the corner of my eye I saw that she had forgotten to pull the zip up on my mini-skirt. I hoped without confidence that she would warn Laura.

Daisy was more Gordon than I gave her credit for. Not only had she Laura and Mick—both as full as the Boyne—hidden in the bedroom but she had relieved Richard of his wine bottle and warned him about Sandra before he got into the living room. And Richard was of course magnificent and rose to the occasion like a real trooper. Sandra, I could see, was impressed, but she seemed even less ready to leave. If anything, the rabbit sank even deeper into our armchair.

"Yes," I could hear Richard saying as I left the room to check the potatoes, "Yes I went to school with Charles Montgomery, George's brother. Charles was quite brilliant, got the science prize every year; studying veterinary science now, I believe."

Daisy was mournfully watching the potatoes.

"Laura and Mick are in the bedroom," she sniffed.

"They won't come out until she has gone. But where is my prince?"

"Romeo, Romeo, where the hell are you?" I comforted her. And with that the doorbell buzzed and Daisy blanched and grabbed my arm—vice-grips.

"I'll get it," she said.

I glimpsed the Muesli prince as he passed the kitchen door *en route* to the living room. He didn't look like a salesman.

"Charlie," said Richard, "Charlie Montgomery, well I never did!"

At this point Mick decided that he had been cooped up in the bedroom quite long enough and descended on the living room, with Laura under one arm and a fistful of mistletoe grasped in his shovel-like paw. He dropped Laura, now giggling weakly, on to Charlie's lap and grabbed the rabbit for a huge slobbery Christmas kiss. Sandra was almost overcome by the fumes of Mick's enthusiasm, and pity almost entered my rationale by the time Laura had got him dragged away.

"Sandra," squeaked Laura, suddenly focusing on the victim. "Sandra Jackson, what are you doing here? Have you come as Daisy's date for the dinner party?"

She turned to Charlie, bemused and amused by the spectacle.

"You mustn't question my sister's sexual preferences,"

she explained solemnly. "Sandra is from Magherafelt, she is a fellow Ulster woman, as such I assume she is here. I can't recall her being invited. But anyway. I take it you are the Muesli prince. We haven't been introduced, most remiss. I am Laura May Gordon and I am delighted to make your acquaintance." She smiled winningly and held out her hand.

"Enchanted," said Charlie and winked at me.

Laura insisted that Sandra stay for dinner.

"No Sandra," she said, "I will not have you turned out in the snow like the Little Matchgirl. You must sit beside Mick, he is as gentle as a pussy-cat really. No, no, I insist, sit beside Mick. He was just excited earlier. I shall sit here beside the Muesli prince."

The wine had a dreadful effect on Charlie. He was on his ear after two glasses and became delightfully funny, telling Daisy she had the most beautiful liquid cow's eyes he had ever seen. Daisy was unsure if this was a compliment or an insult, until he complimented me on the symmetry of my eyebrows. Mick caught on, and lumbering to his feet announced a toast to Laura, who had, he said, "A nice smile, but nicer tits."

Sandra who had drunk an entire glass of Le Piat d'Or on Laura's insistence looked a little faint.

Daisy had forgotten to take the entrails out of the turkey but fortunately Richard, who carved, said nothing about it. I could depend on Richard.

Mick complimented Daisy on her "firm, yet succulent breast" and the "rounded perfection of her thigh." Daisy, missing the sexual innuendoes, was highly flattered.

We had finished the guests' wine before the end of dinner, so I produced some gooseberry wine that gran-gran had made the summer before she died. The gooseberry kicked like a mule and finished off Charlie completely, who retired to the bathroom to splash his face with cold water.

Mick then demonstrated the reason he was four stones overweight by consuming most of the pudding and belching loudly afterwards.

Only Richard, whom I would have trusted with my life, kept his head, held his drink and conducted an intelligent conversation with Sandra. Once I heard the rabbit telling him about Trinity College Christian Union, and when our eyes met across the table I mouthed, "Sorry," at him. He was so calm, so controlled, so utterly rock steady, my hero.

Charlie returned from the bathroom just as Mick was hoisting Laura over his shoulder.

"The night is young," he said, "and I have oats to sow," and he went off to ravish Laura in peace. We heard him fling open her bedroom door, throw her on to the bed. Next came the sound of her battering

him and shouting, "Unhand me, you drunken scut."
Her protests went unheeded, then there was a sudden
silence and she reappeared looking rumpled and
laughing to inform us that Mick had fallen into a
drunken slumber.

Sandra having eaten us out of house and home,
and pried into our privacy, decided to go home.

"Stay a while," begged Laura. "You are mighty
crack, Sandra, I never knew you drank."

Fear enveloped the rabbit. "But I don't," she
stuttered. "Laura, I don't drink."

Laura winked massively.

"Of course you don't," she whispered conspiratorially. "Of course you don't and neither do we."

After Sandra left (was she running?) Mick reappeared and, better behaved now, pulled Laura onto
his knee and conducted a reasonable conversation
with Charlie, who was cuddling Daisy on the sofa.
Daisy looked as if she cuddled men on the sofa all the
time. Only Richard and I sat apart, because we weren't
dating: we were just friends.

CHAPTER SIX

My classmates might have been wearing dinner-jackets but there was no mistaking that they were farmers—only an Ag would pile the empty pint glasses ten high at a formal ball.

We had talked of nothing else but the ball in the flat since coming back after Christmas and had dyed our underwear black in anticipation. It had been raining the afternoon we had done it and we had hung the underwear along the fireplace to dry. Bit embarrassing as Mr Rentokil had called in an un-marked car and caught us unprepared for him, and had seen it.

Daisy had surprised a rat sitting on the top of the fridge, eating our Dunnes Stores 33-pence white loaf. (There was a price war between Dunnes Stores and Quinnsworth at the time.) She had let such a yell out of her, that I had sat bolt upright in bed—our bedroom was beside the kitchen. Through the strangled yells she informed me of our guest. When I shouted at her to shut the kitchen door and not to let the rat into the rest of the house she had sobbed, "I can't: I am standing on a chair."

I am not an animal lover, and I was furious that *Rattus Rattus* had decimated our loaf. I had nothing to make sandwiches with for college.

Richard thought the incident highly amusing, and suggested that we start buying Yellow Pack bread, since rats didn't like the taste of it.

Laura had a reputation for courage—after all she was Mick's girlfriend—and she was elected to search the kitchen and find where the rat had got in. She donned a pair of wellies, drank half a bottle of beetroot wine—found hidden in gran-gran's room after the funeral. She advanced on the kitchen with Mick's hurley stick, but Rattus had disappeared, no doubt scared away by Daisy's yelling and the inhospitable atmosphere.

He returned the next evening to run out from behind the cooker and over Daisy's foot while she was making us toast before bed. Laura was in the kitchen with her, buttering the toast and she flung an ashtray after him but he dashed beneath the fridge. She slammed the kitchen door shut and yelled for me to come and help Daisy move the fridge. She stood poised with the floorbrush to wallop him when he ran out.

The plan worked in that Daisy and I moved the fridge but Daisy's nerves were shattered and, when she saw the rat crouching in the corner, she let a scream out of her and ran out of the kitchen leaving the door open behind her. Rattus saw his chance for escape and darted after her but, instead of following her out of the front door, he leapt into the fireplace in the living room and down the hole in the back. I'd say he was wiping the sweat from his forehead, so close had been the shave.

Well he must have met a nice girl down the back of the fireplace and used a good chat-up line, because we caught them disco dancing in the living room to Kylie the next morning. Mr Rentokil arrived but the only advice he gave us was to get rid of the fridge as it was "the greatest passion-killer" he had ever heard. The fridge rumbled a bit and froze everything but frozen milk was the least of our worries.

Rattus must have been fully occupied with his girlfriend for a while after that because he was only sighted occasionally; he would stick his head out round the fireplace, give us a knowing wink and disappear back to where he came from for more rumpy-pumpy. We considered asking him to pay rent.

As Daisy and Charlie had become an item they were going to the ball together and Mick naturally was bringing Laura. I often wondered if their relationship, which Laura had originally cited as "purely sexual," was still so.

"Helen, honey," she laughed when I asked her, "catch a grip."

I shifted a number of Ags in the weeks before the ball but refused each of them in turn when they asked me to accompany them. It was one thing shifting, quite another to spend the whole evening with the same man. I wanted someone who would entertain me, who wouldn't expect me to be the star the whole evening.

"Have you accepted any of the half dozen delightful young men who asked you to the ball this week?" Richard asked me one Friday, about a week before the ball, when he found me sulking in the Ag common room after a statistics class.

"No."

"What about the 4th Ag whom you shifted last night?" Richard never went to Ag discos but he always knew what I had been up to.

"Oh Richard," I pouted, "I can't spend the entire evening with him. He is interested in nothing but hunting, and Daisy would have a kitten if he was at our table. You know what a rampant anti she is."

"Is Daisy aware that Charlie's family have been Masters of Hounds down the country since Cromwell's time?" Richard smiled.

"No she isn't and she doesn't know that Charlie whips-in for them either," I sighed. Charlie and I had become quite friendly since the night of the dinner party and we often had a cup of tea and a chat when he was waiting for Daisy to get ready to go out with him. Daisy was so in love she sang when she got up in the morning, and she filled everybody's hot water bottle before we went to bed at night.

"Well," said Richard slowly, "It appears then that I shall have to ask you." He was staring fixedly at his hands.

"But I thought that you weren't going to go," I said.

"Oh Helen, Helen," he smiled, "I can't let you take some innocent man to the ball and allow you to eat him alive when I have it in my power to save him."

He stared very hard at me, then smiled. "Would you care to accompany me to the ball, Miss Gordon?"

"I should be delighted," I said and, surprised, I realised that I really meant it.

My sisters and I had a small punch party before the ball, to warm us up. This was the first showing of my Scarlett dress and I felt seductively sluttish as I admired myself in the wardrobe mirror. Richard, of course, didn't comment on it, which was just as well because he would have told me to cover myself if he had said anything. He never did the superior act or the masterful one with me because he knew from experience that I wouldn't listen. I tended to be a law unto myself. Daisy said she thought he looked awfully handsome in his black tie—she looked divine in midnight blue taffeta which mummy had made for her. Mummy was so excited that Daisy had caught herself a boyfriend that she had made the dress a mite more risqué than Daisy normally wore, and when Mick tried to ping her bra-strap and found she wasn't wearing one he slapped Charlie on the back and boomed: "Watch that woman Charlie, she's an animal in bed." And it must be recorded that Daisy had blossomed so convincingly since she had met Charlie that she only laughed at Mick. I think it very unfair that the evening which had started so well should have ended so disastrously.

Richard and I were dancing cheek to cheek and I felt warm and the wine was making me reckless.

Really I thought, sliding closer and idly running my fingers over the back of his neck, really Richard was rather attractive: he was the right height when I wore my high shoes and he held me tight when we were dancing. When Richard danced with me I knew he wasn't wishing himself at the bar, swilling pints and telling dirty jokes. I nuzzled even closer and could feel his breath, soft and warm, on my neck. Any minute he was going to kiss me...

But he didn't.

He jerked up his head and frowned. "Now Helen," he was quite cross, "don't try the seduction scene on me because I am not going to fall for it."

"Richard!" I was speechless.

He stomped off the floor, leaving me standing like a spare part in the middle of everyone else. Slowly I walked back to our table, which was empty and sitting down I watched the whirling dancers. Slowly I became furious with him and, by the end of the slow set, I was spitting mad and ready to go home.

Of course I was going home. I had never been so humiliated in my life. From Richard, Richard Knight, my friend. I couldn't think of an obscenity bad enough, and I left without telling him I was away. I could see him standing at the bar talking to someone, not looking at me. I walked home so fast I had a stitch, and it wasn't until I was boiling the kettle to wash my face that my heart stopped pounding. I simply couldn't believe that he had done it. I was unleashing a tirade of abuse into my diary when the doorbell rang, a well-mannered gentlemanly ring. Richard was on the threshold looking calm, superior, I thought.

"What do you want?" I felt like poking his eyes out.

"I came to see if you got home alright."

I threw a real wobbly on the door step—daddy

and Jennifer would have been proud of me—and called him every bad name I could think of. I called him a toe-rag, a guttersnipe; I think I called him a shithawk as well.

While I was saturating him with insults, he, still calm, picked me up over his shoulder and carried me into the flat and, putting me over his knee, spanked me thoroughly, holding me firmly with one hand and whacking me with the other.

It was pretty painful and I howled for him to stop. I was whimpering when he set me down on my bed and stood up.

"Now," he said still calm. "Now listen to me, Helen, because I enjoyed that performance as much as you did."

Liar! I would have laid bets on it that he had had the time of his life.

"Helen I don't care how many men you seduce, I don't care if you shift the half of Ag but you are not doing the same to me. You destroy everything that loves you."

I thought I was going to cry, and started snivelling unromantically. He softened immediately because though he could handle me in a tantrum, weeping females embarrassed him.

"Will we make up and be friends? Let's just forget what happened," he said. "Scarlett, you harlot, stop pouting and give me a smile."

I smiled weakly and he sat down on the bed beside me.

"Don't come too close," I snapped tartly, "In case I rape you."

He shook his head. "Not now we understand each other."

Poor Rattus. He chose the wrong moment to take his evening stroll to the kitchen. I saw him pattering quietly past the bedroom door, and dashed into the kitchen after him. I had him smashed to pieces before either the rat or Richard realised what I was up to. I was still bashing at him with the floorbrush when Richard arrived in the kitchen, to save either me or the rat, I'm not sure which.

"I pretended it was you," I said.

Rattus's lady-love either died of a broken heart or else found herself another man because she wasn't sighted down the fireplace again.

I'm afraid Richard escalated in my esteem after "The Ball Affair" which I didn't dare tell anyone else about. I classed him as the one that got away.

But it was odd though. Do people always want the thing they can't get?

CHAPTER SEVEN

O ur first lambs were due during the three weeks we were home for Easter. It appeared that the rota daddy had drawn up for checking the ewes included the entire family, not just himself and mummy. Because he had made the rota so complicated nobody could follow it and he usually rose in the middle of the night himself. He always woke everyone in the house when he did.

Jennifer was furious that she should be included in the rota as she said that ewes had been lambing for centuries unassisted and there was no need for her to waste her beauty sleep doing nursemaid. She was probably right too, because the sheep that daddy had bought were from the mountain and had had more pregnancies than even mummy.

Mummy had been excited initially by the prospect of multiple births but as daddy spent more and more time with the sheep and less time with her she became jealous and threatened to cite the sheep as her husband's "mistress" when she divorced him.

The first lamb popped out in the field before lunch

time, which disappointed mummy terribly because she had expected twins from all of them. Perhaps I should add here that mummy hadn't been reared on a farm.

"Are you sure there is not another lamb inside her?" she kept asking daddy over lunch. "Maybe you should do an internal examination to find out?"

She was fascinated by the thought of an "internal examination" and couldn't wait to stick her hand up a ewe's bum to bring new life into the world. She hadn't long to wait. That evening daddy was at the Orange lodge ("If I don't divorce him over the head of the sheep, it will be the Orange order I'll cite.") and I decided to check up on mummy checking up on the ewes. It was just as well that I did because I found her comforting one of the hornies who was in the throes of childbirth and who had her lamb jammed inside her.

"Why didn't you try to get the lamb out?" I asked as she insisted that I roll up my sleeves and do the dirty deed.

"Midwifery is nauseous," was all she said.

So while she comforted the ewe, stroked her head and told her the story of the "Three Little Pigs" I performed major surgery.

"My hand is crushed," I groaned desperately trying to ease one leg forward and ignoring the swollen head which had turned mummy's stomach.

"Forget the hand," mummy barked. "Get the lamb out."

The lamb was huge when I finally eased her out, and on mummy's insistence I groped round inside her again to see if there was a twin. Indeed there was and the little thing wasn't half the size of his sister. The ewe was fairly shook—for that matter so was I— and Jennifer, who had been watching at a safe distance, was dispatched into the house for a bottle of Guinness to resuscitate her.

Mummy had been a teetotaller for years and tended to get on her hobby horse about the evils of drink.

However, there are two requirements for acceptance into the Agricultural faculty in Dublin. One is to be able to dismantle, fix and operate the photocopying machine blindfolded, and the other is to have a healthy appreciation of black stout. Daisy and I had been known to sip the odd glass as confirmation of our acceptance into the faculty. We lectured mummy on its medicinal properties, the yeast, vitamin B content, and the iron and she had taken to drinking it herself. She always drank a glass when she was out because she thought a pint wasn't ladylike. Indeed, even Mick refused to buy me pints in Dublin though he didn't mind how many glasses I drank.

Mummy took to Guinness as a duck takes to water

and proclaimed its virtues to any one who would listen. It lifted headaches, relieved indigestion, made her hair grow faster and her skin tan browner. I heard her musing as to whether she should recommend it to Rachael, the minister's anaemic wife, who always looked tired and washed out.

It said a lot for the ewe that mummy was willing to sacrifice a bottle for her sake. But then again, she preferred draught Guinness to the bottled sort.

That spring a mob of rabbits attacked mummy's shrubs and she swore she wakened at every sunrise to their chomping and munching and that she could see the juice dripping off their chins as they sauntered out of the gardens after a hearty breakfast.

In fact she worked herself up into such a fit one morning that she took the gun out herself to shoot them.

Though by no means a pacifist—she often threw things at daddy—she had a sudden burst of "Thou shalt not..." at the last minute and instead of discharging the shot into the wicked rabbits she aimlessly fired into a row of beech trees in the hope of frightening them off. The rabbits were a tough bunch of bandits and they were unimpressed by their last-minute reprieve. The ungrateful vermin simply chewed the mouthful a little better than before and touched noses conspiratorially.

Mummy's stray shot had, by some mischance of fate, hit and fatally wounded an old crow who had retired to the beech trees many moons before, after a life of robbing strawberry beds and grain fields. How inglorious for the ancient campaigner to be sent west by a woman's bullet. Mummy seemed to think so too for she forgot her vendetta against the other vermin in her self-reproach for the murder of Mr Crow.

Clad in pink plastic rubber gloves and an appropriate funeral face she ceremoniously retrieved Mr Crow from the barbed wire on the top of the slurry lagoon on to which he had fallen and we prepared his last resting place. Sarah supplied a cardboard box, to bury him in, and Jennifer fashioned a cross—she was good at that sort of thing.

His epitaph: Here Lies Mr Crow, Death By Hideous Misadventure.

We all felt as if we had known him personally and grieved as if we had lost a dear and valued friend. Mummy felt his passing most—never having killed anything before, though having often threatened daddy—and resolved never to kill again.

Instead, daddy was posted to the position of Chief Rabbit Slayer. As it was generally believed that the rabbit community had extrasensory perception, a professional assassin such as daddy preferred guerrilla tactics to single combat.

In short, he sniped at them from the dining room window.

I think he did a fine job, three one morning with a single shot—an indication perhaps of the field of a single cartridge. The ones we used, a blind man could hit the eye of a travelling rat.

Daddy's success in killing motionless and defenceless rabbits instilled higher aspirations in him, and it soon became a point of honour with him to send undesirables packing with a shot from the gun from an upstairs window. We effectively dispersed two Jehovah Witnesses this way once. I think they thought the Second Coming had come whether or not they believed in it.

Daddy got too smart one day when he tried the same trick on Ian, the ubiquitous boyfriend, and Sarah sulked with him for a week as she was convinced Ian would never be back and life as she knew it was over. In the end daddy had to greet Ian at the front door, and extend the hand of friendship to him to prove he felt no animosity to his prospective son-in-law. Sarah was studying for A Levels at this time but she couldn't care less if she passed or failed them as she thought of nothing but marrying Ian and going to live with him in a three-bedroomed brand new semi in a cul-de-sac in a Belfast suburb. Ian would do the gardening and she would keep her double-glazed windows spotless. They would have endless supplies of hot water, a daughter called Rosemary and dainty lace curtains so the neighbours couldn't see in.

We all thought she had flipped but he did give her a massive Roses Easter egg. The rest of us had to make do with creme eggs bought by mummy.

On Good Friday over dinner Laura broke the news that she was going to stay with daddy's cousins in America for the summer on a J1 student visa. No one, not even me, knew that she had planned and organised the entire thing herself. Daddy looked dumbstruck and stopped chewing while he digested the information.

"Do they know yet?" he finally asked.

"Oh yes, daddy," said Laura, "I wrote to them over Christmas and they wrote back to say that they would love to have me. They have a waitressing job lined up for me in the restaurant their son manages. They asked for you in the letter."

She said that to flatter daddy's vanity and to soften the blow of her leaving.

"But I'll miss you," he said finally. Poor daddy! Laura was the only female in the house who went willingly to the Twelfth of July celebrations with him every year. Laura, his brown-eyed girl, who had carried the strings on the banner until she had left primary school. He still bought her a rosette every year with either "No Surrender" or "Remember 1690" on it. She had them pinned on her bedroom curtains, and I think she gave one to Mick for a birthday present when he was 21. She had given daddy Union Jack shorts last Christmas.

"It's educational, daddy," Laura said. "I really feel I ought to avail of such an opportunity to visit our colonial relatives. Maybe they can be persuaded to come over more often and visit you then."

This also pleased daddy but it wasn't the sort of talk mummy wanted to hear. Daddy's American cousins were terribly grand, having lived the American dream, and all of them had become top-line bankers. I suppose mummy thought Derryrose with its rotting window frames and uneven floorboards rather the poor relation. Lee, the son who managed the restaurant, must have been the black sheep of the family in comparison to the others.

On Easter Sunday that year the weather suggested Barbados not Northern Ireland and daddy decided to take us to Portstewart strand for the day. I rose early to make sandwiches; Daisy spent half the morning hunting out our swimsuits—mummy had tidied them away and couldn't remember where—and Jennifer and daddy fought and consequently sulked because each thought he/she could load the car better than the other.

Making sandwiches was a major operation on these excursions and not the ten-minute task enjoyed in other households. Daddy wouldn't eat mayonnaise, mummy was the only one who wanted egg in her sandwiches, Sarah didn't like tomatoes, Jennifer would eat nothing but crunchy peanut butter—the list of demands was endless.

The peanut butter and egg sandwiches had to be packed separately because both tainted the other sandwiches, and no one could abide the taste of peanut butter but Jennifer. She had the disgusting habit of spreading her toast with peanut butter and then using the same knife in the margarine tub, so contaminating everything. (We ate margarine not butter because it was cheaper, not because of health considerations.)

As Jennifer and daddy were still sulking and Daisy remembered that she had forgotten to go to the loo after fifteen minutes on the road I looked out of the window and pretended that my family didn't belong to me.

However, a pit-stop to relieve Daisy, and bags of crisps for both daddy and Jennifer and everybody was friends again, and by the time we reached the strand we were all singing, "She'll be coming round the mountain when she comes." The National Trust man taking the money must have thought we were going round the bend.

As a united family front we raced into the sea and daddy, getting his toes wet, and remembering at the last minute that he was on the wrong side of fifty, raced back out again and dozed in the Morris like an Old-Aged Pensioner, while the rest of us swam until we were blue with cold.

"Good job they breed us tough in the North," mummy commented, her teeth chattering. She then slapped brown vinegar over us saying, "The Fish and Chip crowd that go to Spain every year would love you smelling like this."

The couple in the red Astra next to us didn't think so and moved further up the beach. They had bright orange suntans which led us to suspect that they had just returned from the Costa Del Sol.

Our first feeding revealed that I had forgotten to pack tea-bags and I was unceremoniously packed off to scrounge a bag from three middle-aged women two cars to the left. They were still wearing their Sunday skirts. (I suppose either you are a pagan like my mother who had been up the sandhills spying on canoodling couples, or a nice modest wee woman who preserved Sunday Observancy precepts even while being a heathen on the beach on a Sunday afternoon.)

The middle-aged women were very kind and gave me some sugar too (which I had also forgotten). I took them over some of the chocolate cake that Sarah had baked, later.

"That's a nice big girl," I heard one comment as I left. She had been daring enough to discard her frilly blouse for a suntop and waspishly I hoped her sunburn would hurt like hell later on in the evening. "Big girl," indeed. I felt like spitting.

Parading the Promenade on Sunday night is part of the mating ritual of all Presbyterians, and as Sarah was the only daughter to have what mummy optimistically termed a "marrying job" relationship we were dispatched to walk up and down the Prom with the intention of attracting the attention of some nice suitable young men.

The nice suitable young men sat in cars along the double lines to disguise the fact that they had short legs, fat bums and red shoes.

An elderly lady wearing the most fuddy of all fuddy-duddy hats was performing beneath the War Memorial opposite Morelli's Ice Cream Parlour.

"Standards are slipping," she bellowed as, half-naked, the five of us sauntered past. Collectively, we were wearing less clothing than one of the nice suitable young ladies, holding hymn books, who were standing behind the fuddy-duddy hat.

"Do you think," said Jennifer, "that if we gave her a couple of quid between us, she would take the hat off, and buy herself an ice-cream?"

"Leave her alone," said Sarah. "She probably has nothing else to do on a Sunday night. Everyone else her age is married."

"Or dead," I said.

"Or in Homes for the Bewildered," said Daisy.

We weren't real heathens, of course. If we had been heathens we would have been playing Space Invaders in Portrush but we weren't committed to Street Evangelism either.

We did our Prom tour of duty and daddy bought us an ice-cream as compensation.

The perfect end to the day.

I didn't care if I never went back to Dublin. Laura on the way home claimed to be desperate to get back to Mick's big hands—even our Easter Saturday "Girls Night Out" couldn't compare with his shovels. Daisy, too, looked forward to her reunion with Charlie. I felt a bit left out in all this romancing, and talked to daddy about sheep lambing instead.

CHAPTER EIGHT

L aura left for America at the end of June and we all cried for precisely ten minutes, then promptly forgot about her. It's out of sight, out of mind at Derryrose.

In July I made thirty-two pots of raspberry jam and picked the gooseberries to make wine. Now that gran-gran was dead, the recipes and the responsibility for them were left to me.

Like all men daddy believed himself an expert in all fields including that of jam-making and he supervised the first fruit-picking of the season. When I say supervised, I mean that he sat on the stone wall surrounding the raspberry canes, a burnt sun-hat on his head and gave orders as to which raspberries were ripe enough to pick and which weren't. He did this by eating handfuls of the fruit we girls picked and by criticising us when we stopped for a rest. He would have made an effective slave-driver as he lacked even the rudiments of courtesy and diplomacy. He insulted Jennifer and Sarah so viciously the first day that they never ventured into the garden again to help me.

"Lacking the backbone," he diagnosed of Daisy who had endured his criticisms for the longest but who had eventually escaped with a lame excuse I don't remember now.

"That's what education does to women," he continued. "Makes them feeble."

I knew that it didn't even occur to him to help me. The approach of the Glorious Twelfth has this effect on many normally unassuming Orangemen. I was used to daddy's personality change—in the month of July he acquired the persona of a military commander and bossed the lives out of his "platoon" as he called us. The platoon he had press-ganged into enforced labour in the fruit gardens had revolted, but it was enough that I was still there to give orders to. When he forgot to do the Supreme Commander act he entertained me with the tall tales his Orange friends and he had told the night before while they sat up guarding the arch against Fenian attack. Every night since the arch had been erected, daddy, fortified with a hip-flask of whiskey, set off with his shotgun to sit in Ballyronan with the arch, and I suspect, pray for a bit of excitement. If Fenians had decided to burn the arch, symbol of Protestant supremacy, I doubt there was much the Loyal Orangemen could have done, shotguns or not. It entertained them the way Santa Claus or waiting for a birthday entertains a child.

Daddy supervised my boiling of the jam too. The minute he came into the kitchen mummy, who hates him at this time of the year, because he ignores her, escaped outside. She spent a lot of her time with the notorious Ruth Paisley and often walked the roads of home in the evenings while daddy prepared his hip-flask for the night's operations. Daddy hated her walking round the roads as he said it seemed as if she were looking for a man, which mummy said she was. He suggested that Daisy and I go instead as it looked as if no one was going to take us. Charlie had never been presented at Derryrose and mummy suspected that he was a figment of Daisy's imagination and not a real man at all. And as Charlie was in England all summer on seeing practice he couldn't reveal himself and dispel her suspicions.

Because it wasn't worth the effort of arguing with daddy I followed his instructions to the letter about boiling the jam. I was not overly shocked therefore when the final product had the consistency of thin soup.

"It's a bit runny," I commented as we gloomily stared into the boiling pan.

"Nonsense!" Daddy rallied bravely—keeping up the morale of the troops is the function of a Supreme Commander, even in the face of domestic disaster.

"It's just a little soft, Helen, if it comes to the bit I will drink it all myself, with a straw."

The soup jam was carefully concealed in a massive jar at the back of the cupboard and daddy changed tactics for the next batch. He insisted that I boil and boil and boil it and we squeezed the juice of umpteen lemons into the boiling mixture.

"Oh," said daddy gleefully, "I just know that it is going to set this time." I could imagine him as a child licking the baking bowl after gran-gran made a cake, and opening and closing the oven to see if it was ready.

The jam set with the consistency of concrete, black, sticky and unpalatable. Daddy blamed the lemons, then the raspberries ("There must have been pesticides on them.") and finally me.

"You mustn't have done it properly," he wailed. "My mother never made as awful jam as this."

"Your mother never had you telling her what to do," I heard Jennifer mutter, having come indoors just in time to hear daddy's last remark. Jennifer was very cheeky but mummy had long ago decided that her behaviour was hereditary, caused by a mutant gene passed on from daddy's side of the family. No matter how often she was smacked, she was, if anything, worse behaved afterwards. Sometimes she was even worse than daddy. And because their personalities were so alike and therefore completely incompatible they suffered rather than enjoyed each other's company. And everyone else suffered listening to them alternately arguing and sulking.

I suggested that we hid the concrete jam under a pile of tins in the bin so mummy wouldn't see it and throw a fit. But daddy was terrified that she would discover it and scorn him, so he dug a hole in the field beside the house to bury the evidence. He had to bury both saucepan and contents, because they refused to be separated, and he had burned the arse out of the boiling pan. I suppose the jam should have had a grave beside Mr Crow with an appropriate headstone and epitaph but we didn't think of that at the time. The excitement of jam-making waned somewhat in daddy after the initial chaos, and left to my own devices I made reasonable jam unsupervised. Daisy promptly regained interest once daddy was removed from the scene and we even went so far as to cover the pots with checked cloth like the pictures in the women's magazines.

Once the jam-making was completed the gooseberries were ripe enough for wine production. Daisy pretended to help me pick the gooseberries but she hated the thorns on the bushes and always created excuses to get out of it. Her most credible excuse was that of the postman's arrival. When the postman stops at Derryrose everybody runs to see who has got a letter. Everybody except mummy who says all her letters come in brown envelopes and demand money.

Daisy always seemed to be waiting for a letter from Charlie, always expecting and always being woefully disappointed when the long-anticipated letter didn't come. Seeing her woebegone expression and watching her listless tread back to the gooseberries I became afraid that the wonderful Charlie, the Muesli prince, was actually a member of the B category of manhood. But I shrank from asking her because I hated becoming involved in anyone's problems. I usually ended up worrying more than the person with the problem. Of course, when one of Charlie's infrequent epistles did arrive she was at high doh for days afterwards and mummy was nice to everyone because she felt released from the stigma of an impending spinster daughter. She didn't think Daisy would ever catch another man if she let Charlie get away.

Sarah ran fastest to the post van the day her A Level results came out and was intensely disappointed when she discovered that she had done well enough to be accepted to Stranmillis College in Belfast for teacher training.

"But I don't understand," I said. "Did you want to fail them?"

We were up in her bedroom which she shared

with Daisy and which had pink curtains and pink wallpaper and fluffy toys all over the pink bedspread. Sarah had been crying into her pink pillowcase since the results had come out.

"Of course I wanted to fail," she sobbed, looking fragile and delicate through her tears. "If I had failed Ian and I could have got married. But now I have to learn to be a teacher instead."

Unaware of Sarah's nuptial scheming Ian was delighted she had done so well and took her out to dinner. Starved for big feeds in fancy restaurants the rest of us waited up until she came home to enjoy the experience through her. We were disgusted that she had not brought the bone of Ian's steak home for the dogs and that she had not eaten pudding.

"I read somewhere that ladies never eat pudding," she defended herself.

"Really," said Jennifer with scathing sarcasm.

Laura sent us two letters from America.

In the first she said she liked Lee because he made her laugh. It appears that one Sunday at lunch Lee had farted really loudly.

"Lee," chided his mother Lee Ann, "Lee behave, there are young people in the house," meaning Laura, to which Lee replied:

"So they don't fart then in Ireland, Laura?"

In her second letter she wrote to say that the

cousins had taken her to an open air concert to hear *The Planets* but she was so tired (having been out pounding Guinness the night before) that she fell asleep at the end of the first movement and dreamed she was being sacrificed to the beat of totem drums.

Donald and Lee Ann concluded she wasn't a lover of classical and sent Lee with her to Tina Turner which she said was awesome. The way the letter was worded I wasn't sure if she meant Lee or Tina.

What made the summer for me was the fact that I wasn't going back to Dublin in September. Agricultural Science students at UCD have a practical year to complete before entering their third year. They say this is the reason the Dublin Ag Sci degree is the best.

The practical year can either be completed by the sweat of the brow on the approved farm or by intelligence and cunning in agricultural college. Daddy chose the latter for me as he said no daughter of his was going to kill herself working for any man on an approved farm. Having a chauvinist for a father has its compensations at times. Because the Ag college I was to attend was quite close to home I could take a bus back to Derryrose every Wednesday afternoon, if I wanted to, as well as at the weekends. This consoled Jennifer, now the last daughter to be left at home, as she visualised me diminishing the crescendo of tension she would have built up round herself throughout the week. What she really meant was that mummy would shout at me and not her.

"It's bad when they are fighting," she said of our parents, "but it's worse when they are all lovey-dovey."

For Laura's homecoming daddy killed the fatted mountain ewe. He looked really funny with a sheet wrapped round him following instructions from an illustrated manual and warning us to tell no one what he was up to, as home butchery was illegal. Not even the threat of jail could deter him from this offering to his beloved firstborn on her return. Laura came home at the end of the summer. She was pink with sunburn and really fat.

"The food was awesome," she said over the homecoming dinner. "Lee let me eat as much as I wanted in the restaurant because in America they think Ireland is a Third World country." She said she had read a newspaper article where an Irish child on holiday in America was overcome, on being given a cheese sandwich.

"But Laura," said Sarah, "We took cheese sandwiches to school for years."

Which was true because Sarah never exaggerated.

"And they have the best ice-cream," said Laura, "and muffins, and hot dogs and a burger place on every corner the way they have a pub on every corner here."

One woman in the restaurant had told her she had the face of a nun (Daddy snorted). Laura said that the woman had meant it as a compliment thinking a nice Irish girl would be thrilled by such a remark. She had been incensed. Her trip too, to the Niagara Falls had been ruined because the attendant for the *Maid of the Mist* had charged her as an "under-12."

"It's not my fault," she stormed, "that my nose peels and I look like Shirley Temple with my hair tied back."

Mummy tried to comfort her by saying that it would be a blessing for her in years to come, to have youthful features.

"What do I care what I look like when I get old?" Laura had yelled back rudely and forgetting herself added, "The men all thought I wasn't over the age of consent."

"Well," said Sarah smoothly to cover up the first major gaffe Laura had ever made in front of our parents, "Well that's probably just as well. I read somewhere that American men are very persistent about that sort of thing."

That was something I had to say for Sarah, she always kept her head in an emergency. She then changed the subject completely.

"I suppose no one told you I almost electrocuted myself on Friday night?"

Having passed her driving test over the summer, and being Sarah, she always cleaned the Morris outside and in before she drove anywhere, even into Magherafelt under cover of dark. The continuous cleaning worried daddy a little because the Morris had more rust than paint, and a power hose would have killed the car completely.

While she had been admiring her reflection in the rear view mirror she had stuck the arm of the vacuum cleaner into a basin of water she had used to clean the hubcaps.

"No one knows why there wasn't a sizzling noise and a charred carcass," she laughed. I had read a novel once where the heroine had laughter like "silver bells." That was how Sarah laughed, silver bells.

"Born under a lucky star as well as a beautiful one," smiled Daisy. Daisy actually enjoyed sharing the pink fluffy bedroom with Sarah and claimed that Sarah wasn't half as boring as we stereotyped her. This was only because Sarah admired Daisy's flower pictures and listened to her Chopin recitals, and endured hours of Daisy mooning about Charlie.

"It concerns me," she said once to me, "that his letters are so infrequent and so factual."

"You mean you read them?" I asked, scandalised.

Sarah didn't do dishonest things like that. Laura maybe, Jennifer certainly, or mummy if she was bored with *The Quiet Man* or *Gone with the Wind* but not Sarah, who carried most of the morals of Derryrose on her slender shoulders. "Certainly not," said Sarah firmly. "Daisy reads them to me, because she is also concerned about his lack of emotion."

It didn't bode well I thought that the letters were so "factual" that she could actually read them out aloud. I wouldn't even read Richard's letters out loud and it went without saying that there was nothing intimate in them, just stories he knew would make me laugh, and caustic character sketches of his neighbours. They were intimate in that they were written for me and I certainly didn't wish to share them with any of my sisters, even Daisy who thought the sun shone out of his eyes.

"Hasn't Laura got heavy?" said Sarah suddenly as we washed up afterwards. "I think I have some information in a magazine I bought last week about losing weight—I shall hunt it out for her."

Sarah was always buying herself feminist glossies which conflicted somewhat with her womanly attitudes. I usually read the novel extracts and short stories. Jennifer, I know, read her horoscope and the Problem Page (though she said the problems in the *Sun* were better).

"Does Ian realise you read that stuff?" Ian never struck me as a New Age man, or what ever it was the woman in the magazines demanded from their men.

"Oh I don't read the articles," she said, "I just look at the pictures."

The magazine article was duly found (Sarah was very tidy and never lost anything), and presented to Laura who read it out loud to me then burned it in the range.

"The best way to lose weight in problem areas is to combine a healthy diet with regular exercise. Reduce your fat intake by cutting out margarine, butter, hard cheese and cream. Use only skimmed milk, eat only minimal amounts of red meat and avoid excess salt and sugar. Satisfy your appetite with wholemeal bread, pasta, and baked potatoes. Be sure to eat plenty of fresh fruit and vegetables and get protein from white fish and white meat."

"Good grief," said Laura, "I would rather satisfy my appetite with a Mars Bar sandwich. Anyway I think the thinner you are the more boring you become. Sarah is skinny and she is deathly boring."

"I suppose if you were skinny Lee wouldn't love you any more?" Subtly, since she had come home I had been trying to find out about her relationship with the awesome Lee.

"If I was skinny, he wouldn't even see me," she

laughed. Her face lit up when she talked about Lee but she was emphatic that they were just "good friends."

"Just good friends" is a very misleading remark.

"He says he is coming to visit me some time," she added, almost as a footnote.

CHAPTER NINE

Extracts of letters composed by Helen Gordon to Richard JF Knight:

October

Oh Richard,

Is it as terrible for you to soil your hands in manual labour as it is for me to pretend that I am sixteen again? Agricultural college is only two weeks old and already I have aged by centuries. Horrible small fat boys who leer at me constantly and beastly food science students with their superior smiles and their "Come and sit with us, little girl." The third evening I was gloomily sipping tepid tea and admiring the only nail left on my left hand when two of them joined me. Initially I assumed they pitied me, sitting alone, shy, nervous, perhaps timid, and they spoke gently yet patronisingly at me:

"How many CSEs have you?"

They smiled at each other when I said I didn't have any. "A real thicko," they were thinking and I disliked their attitude so I said, "I have 8 GCEs though."

First they thought I was joking, then they remembered I was too stupid to think up such a whopper.

"I have four A Levels," I added, because I liked the look of puzzlement on their faces.

"What are you doing here?"

The big fat one with a signet ring on his little finger stopped stuffing quiche and chips into his mouth so intense had become his interest.

"Well it's a sort of break from my university degree."

I felt rather mean afterwards as I haven't burdened anyone else with all that info. The small fats see me as seventeen and a bit temperamental (they attribute this to my hair colouring), and so long as none of the lecturers blows my cover I reckon I might just survive.

Actually I rather impressed the little boys because I knew what a vasectomy was. Daisy left for Dublin this evening, and I almost wished that I was going with her. What do I have to look forward to? An 8am start in the pighouses, and they smell like Hell. Daisy washed her hair last night, and when it hadn't started to dry after two hours she remembered that she hadn't washed the conditioner off. How will she cope without me to look after her.

Laura will have a breakdown mothering her; you know how useless she is and how unreliable Laura is.

And as for Charlie Montgomery, I don't care if you went to school with his brother, Richard he is firmly B category. I don't know what he wrote in his last letter but whatever it was she ripped all his letters up on Saturday night, cried her eyes out, and then stuck them back together again on Sunday before she left for Dublin. She wouldn't let mummy and daddy take her down in the car as she wants an excuse to come home next weekend. Laura is naturally furious because she has some sort of psychological thing about sitting on a bus. No matter how often she goes to the loo before she gets on to the bus, you can guarantee that she will be bursting ten miles up the road.

Oh Richard why is life so complicated today? I swept the pighouses and quoted Keats's "Ode to Autumn" over and over to myself last week but what "mists and mellow fruitfulness" did I experience? I was moving a thick-witted, bad-tempered sow to the service house and would she leave her pen? I asked nicely, then I threatened her, ("You are going for bacon," I told her.) I shouted at her, I pulled her tail and when she still wouldn't budge I bashed her over the head with a shovel. I *felt like a child batterer afterwards, and couldn't have tea. Things can only get better...*

November

Richard, Richard,

There are normal people on my course after all. And I reversed a tractor and trailer perfectly and it has stopped raining after a fortnight of continuous drip, drip, drip. I cried off "sick" for a couple of days after the last suicidal note I sent you and visited Aunt Maisie in Donegal...

We had a "civilised sherry" in the evening before dinner and a "small port" afterwards, and before bed she read me the dirty bits in Hamlet. We had afternoon tea at four sharp, Earl Grey, of course, with a slice of lemon. We drank it from a grotesque tea-set, which is a bit of an heirloom, as Aunt Maisie's Sunday school class presented it to her sixty-four years ago when she gave up teaching to go to Queen's.

"Worthless darling, but such sentimental value."

She then told me I had lost all my feminine curves, and men don't like thin women. No wonder she hasn't married, she is as thin as a stick. She says I should wear lipstick all the time as "it adds definition to your face, dear." I recall you calling me a jezebel once Richard, because I touched up my face at lunchtime at college.

When we weren't getting tight on her vast store of wines and listening to her endless music (I got the job of winding up the gramophone), we walked in her garden and she was delighted that I took an interest in it. I'm in line for the inheritance now I should think. I felt like such a hypocrite when I went back to Ag college and the lecturers were concerned for my health.

"Were you sick or were you skiving? one of the mountainy men asked. They are the demigods of the course, and you are one of the lads if you are in their gang. I'm honoured to be spoken to. I didn't answer Cyril's question and he jabbed me in the ribs with his elbow and said: "You sly piece, I always knew you were sly."

I'm sure that the jab was meant to be a friendly gesture but I was convinced that a lung was punctured at the time.

Socially, there is a tiny glimmer of hope at the end of my dark tunnel since the (late) arrival of another girl to the course. She is really something else. One of the mountainy men, Albert, piddled in her wellie boot (just to see how she would react). She poured it over him and kicked him in the groin, and swore so much that I blushed for Albert who is half-innocent, I think. I am quite afraid of her

though I believe her to be no more than seventeen.
Her room is next door to mine, and she plays her
Bat Out of Hell album constantly. I have heard it
so often I am starting to enjoy it, a change from
Vivaldi anyway.

Daisy is horribly unhappy, Richard. If you are
ever in Dublin, please call out and see her. She and
Charlie are undergoing divorce proceedings. I always
knew he was B category, far too bossy for little
Daisy. I know she is taller than me but that isn't
the issue. She can't fight and she loves too much,
she is capable of dying of a broken heart.

November 19

Dear R,

The Monster of Ag. college, Sylvia to her friends,
and I, have become friends. She invited me into her
"sanctuary" for a cup of tea last night. This was
rather risky of us you know, as large electrical
appliances (including hairblowers) aren't allowed
into the rooms. I have to hide my kettle, tape player
and wireless when I leave the room. I disgraced
myself badly by sitting on the tea-bag and staining
the bum of my white jeans. She is quite a normal
girl really, cursing and violence aside, and she got
three sentences out without the f-word in any of
them. I attribute her language to shyness though

Laura suggested a Freudian theory related to sexual repression. I shouldn't class Sylvia as repressed, she had Albert in her room all last night. (I met him on the stairs this morning en route to breakfast, and he looked as if he hadn't had a wink of sleep—he was wearing a big penis happy head.) Sylvia says she needs something to help her sleep the beds are so hard. I haven't resorted to taking a toy-boy yet, still comforting myself with a hot water bottle.

Gloom and darkest torment pervade our happy home atmosphere in Derryrose. Wailing from a tormented soul (Jennifer) and gnashing of teeth (mummy) greeted my homecoming on Friday night. I had had a rough afternoon chasing a harem of half-wild Angus cows and their handsome short-legged bull for a brucellosis test, and was not prepared either physically or mentally for the ensuing agonies.

It seems mummy had an uncharacteristic burst of maternal nostalgia on Wednesday night and went up to Jennifer's bedroom to tuck her in and kiss her goodnight. In she burst on the unsuspecting Jennifer—mummy never knocks as she lives in hope that she will catch one of us up to no good. She caught Jennifer enjoying a cigarette and a quiet glass of gin. And if this wasn't provocation enough Jennifer's room (which had belonged to our sainted gran-gran) is papered with posters of naked men. I slept in there one night and had a gruesome nightmare from which I wakened in a cold sweat. I attribute it to the anatomy surrounding me. So mummy freaked and is convinced Jennifer is the Whore of Babylon and there was a conference and talk of sending her to Aunt May on an extended visit—Jennifer has threatened to slit her throat if she has to go—her own throat, not Aunt May's...

Aunt May is mummy's widowed sister; we reckoned her husband died to escape her she is so pious. She has one daughter Tracy who is about my age. Tracy was reciting huge chunks of Scripture while I was reciting Hickory Dickory Dock. Her closest friend is Sandra Jackson. Mummy hopes Aunt May's deathly small-talk and aseptic housekeeping will catalyse a blinding conversion in the pagan J, as Saul was converted on the road to Damascus. I however envisage a nervous break-down—and the murder of the plump unobtrusive Tracy, whom Jennifer despises. My prayers aren't for Jennifer's exorcism but for the abatement of mummy's temper.

Daisy's eyes looked as if they had been crying for ever when she and Laura came home for Christmas. Vast violet shadows stained the pallor of her once pretty face—the way I look after a rough night on the tiles, with mascara seeping through patchy make-up, stale from the night before. (I was a notorious believer in imprinting hypoallergenic foundation on pillow cases.) But my eyes would be bright from a night of excitement; Daisy's were dull. She asked me if she could join Laura and me on our "whoring and touring" expeditions over the festive season which distressed me somewhat; Daisy on principle didn't approve of the turnover rate of young men that Laura and I dealt with. So I confronted her with the Charlie issue. She smiled wanly and said that from henceforth Charlie was as one "dead, buried and forgotten about." I thought there was a hollow ring in her voice when she said it.

Laura and she were still in the flat in Palmerston Road sharing with a friend of Richard's called Elisabeth. Laura said that if she ever saw Charlie Montgomery again she was going to head-butt him or if Mick was with her, he was going to do it for her. (Mick was still on the scene, his hands were larger than Lee's.)

"Daisy thinks her life is over," said Laura, "and that is fine: she can have a broken heart if she wants, but I am suffering as much as she is. She cries herself to sleep every night and plays that dreadful love-song music on the wireless all the time. Elisabeth is always out so it's me who has to listen to her and my sympathy dried up after the first week."

"But what actually happened between them?" I demanded, wishing I could have been there to offer Daisy a shoulder to cry on.

"Who knows?" snorted Laura. "Who cares?"

Whoring and touring to be a pleasurable and rewarding pastime requires strategic organisation and so Daisy needed initiation. When Laura and I frequented student establishments we dressed, spoke and acted like the students we were; at the cattle markets in Portrush, however, we trussed ourselves as brainless bimbos and sold ourselves to the best-looking bidder. My preferences lay with the students where I could communicate using words of more than one syllable but there was a certain appealing cultural diversity in being treated as a lump of flesh.

Daisy initially found the transaction unpleasant but there was little student life at Christmas so it was through necessity not choice that she apprenticed as a bimbo. The first evening she joined us she was wearing the frock she had worn to the school dance aged fifteen. She would have looked appropriate at a prayer meeting, or a Women's Institute cake sale.

"Hang loose, baby," I advised and bullied her into a creation of Laura's which though not quite slut standard was getting there.

"You aren't Margaret Florence Gordon, Agricultural undergraduate, flower presser and Chopin pianist tonight. You are another woman entirely, wilder and more artificial, and you are going to beat the bimbos at their own game."

"But Helen," she was being reasonable, "How can I enjoy the company of a man who is only interested in me because I am hanging out of a skin-tight dress, I am not interested in men who have no soul and no compatibility."

"Honey," I drawled, "You aren't out there searching for a real man, because there won't be any. Real men don't frequent cattle markets."

Why did Daisy seek explanations for this type of behaviour? I was reticent at the best of times to explain my motives for anything but I did appreciate that she required justification.

"Look Daisy," I said, "tonight is a game, you will shift someone you neither respect nor like as a man but he will be hellishly attractive and attentive and he will try to entertain you for the evening. And you will go with the flow because you know you need never see him again; and you can talk to him all night but he need never know you. He is a flitting piece of passion for you as you are for him. It is shallow and meaningless but when you master the game it's fun; no one gets hurt because you don't go

hoping or expecting for a relationship or intimacy."
I thought I had explained adequately given that I
had never analysed the thing before.

"A game," she repeated. "But Richard isn't a game
is he?"

She had huge dark eyes and they seemed bigger
when she stared into mine, and the question, so
quietly and deliberately asked, demanded a truthful
answer.

"No Richard isn't a game, but don't ask me what
he is because I don't know."

I didn't enjoy thinking of Richard on evenings
such as these because pictures of him invariably
popped into my head at inopportune moments. I
once tried to imagine him at a cattle market, propping
up one of the mushroom tables and eyeing up the
women but it was so ridiculous a scenario that I had
given up. Richard couldn't haunt me on a bimbo
night because he didn't belong on a night like that.

Thankfully Daisy didn't try to probe the "Richard
and Helen" enigma further and submitted herself to
my choice of make-up, which, like the dress, was also
contrived and artificial. When I had finished with
her she was stunning in a glamour girl type of way,
and the last traces of flower presser and Chopin pianist
disintegrated when I piled her fair hair on the top of
her head and pulled a few curls forward round her

face.

"Theoretically you should be wearing a gallon of hairspray," I commented squirting some of the ozone-friendly variety in her ear by accident. I was very impressed with the job I had made of her.

Then Jennifer, who had been given Christmas parole from the doghouse, decided at the last minute to join us. She changed her mind when I insisted that she wear a dress.

"And look like a woman," she scoffed. "No thank you."

The last time she had gone out with us she had told someone that she was a plasterer and had come up from Fermanagh in an articulated lorry. She had spent the rest of the evening dodging him because he thought she had been chatting him up. She was great fun to go out with but not on a "whoring and touring" night.

CHAPTER TEN

T he night began much the same as it began in every nightclub in every town. House music ("all noise and no tune," to quote Daisy) pounded away and we watched for talent with the detached interest of a cat as she watches a mouse before pouncing.

"You are looking too intelligent," I growled at Daisy, who promptly adopted an inane hangdog expression—the type Sarah wore when she was with Ian.

Naturally no move was traditionally made by the "men" until the first and only set of smoochy records. As "Je t'aime" gasped, writhed and groaned from the speakers, three identical sports coats, striped shirts and loud ties approached and asked us to dance. The attire included white sports socks and shoulder pads that would have given Woody Allen the breadth of Rambo. My set of shoulder pads got into the over-the-top passion business immediately we reached the dance floor which, even as a bimbo, I couldn't condone so I brusquely told him to lay off and stop pawing at me. This he took as a come-on and because

I hate being with a man whose breath smells of dogfood—due to flat beer on an empty stomach—I flounced off the floor in a bit of a sulk.

"Would you like to dance?"

I didn't bother looking, and without thinking snapped:

"If you think you can manhandle me just because there is a slow record playing you can think again." I was still in a bit of a flap after the previous encounter.

There was a burst of manly laughter. I jerked my head up in surprise. Dammit, it was Hugh Stewart, still fiendishly attractive, and probably the only man in the place not wearing a stripy shirt.

"I won't touch you if you are determined to remain untouchable," he was saying, "but there is little point in us dancing."

He was smiling and my stomach went flippity-flop convincingly. He wasn't escaping so I slipped my hand on to his arm and purred: "Changed my mind, let's dance."

I started my bimbo act once I got to the dance floor but he laughed again and said, "Now, temperamental lady, don't disappoint me and cover up your real self again."

"But I was trying to be a bimbo," I pouted which delighted him even more.

"Yeah, I was watching you earlier with the guy in

the striped shirt. I wondered if you would submit to such an octopus. He seemed pretty determined."

"You were pretty observant," I said sarcastically. I could afford to be sarcastic when I was in his arms. "Pity you couldn't have done the decent thing and rescued me."

"Not I," that infectious laugh again, "I left my white charger at home."

Oh Hugh was lovelier by the minute and I was even more attracted to him than when I was fourteen. He informed me that he was now a student of life— having taken a First degree a couple of years ago— and was at the cattle market to find a bimbo.

"I wanted a compliant obedient one though," he teased, and when he kissed me I half wished he was a groper. I shouldn't have fought him off as fast as Mr Stripy Shirt. Laura and Daisy remained with their clones. Laura was a practised hand in the One-Night-Shift Affair and escaped without any chance of repercussions. Poor Daisy, rookie as she was, got herself a date. Derek thought he was on to a good thing.

"He just launched himself at me," she explained as we drove home. It was pouring but Hugh's kisses were warm on my lips and as I had the car window rolled down to stay awake the rain spray was refreshing on my face. Truthfully, I was a bit giddy from the encounter.

"I hadn't even a chance to duck," Daisy continued. "I mean, when Mick makes a grab at you he at least gives you the opportunity to escape. Not so with Derek, he was all business, you understand."

I understood only too well and Laura was groaning audibly from the back seat.

"Daisy," she moaned, "You have a lot to learn girl."

"It was such a remarkable incident, remarkable, and not altogether unpleasant, you know. Just a bit surprising and very efficient. Reminded me of a combine harvester."

Derek phoned the next evening, and arrived for Daisy in a flashy black Capri with furry dice hanging from the window and a sticker on the back saying, "Sex bomb on board."

She was home again at 11pm on the dot and burst into my bedroom flushed and agitated. Laura and I had been playing chess and discussing Lee, who was to visit in February. Daisy flopped into the armchair by the window and slapped her forehead dramatically.

"How could I?"

It transpired that Derek, true to the nature of his culture, had performed in the way that all plumbers in flashy cars performed.

"I suggested that we go to the lough shore," said

Daisy, "as it was such a clear night and the stars look beautiful reflected on the water—after all what else can one do on a Sunday night? And Derek refused point-blank to come into the house. I suppose I don't blame him for that but we might have been a normal household for all he knew.

"Anyway we got to the lough shore and he stopped the car. I was about to suggest we walk up the bay and watch the reflection of the stars when he tipped my chair back, the way they do in the dentist's. I didn't know what he was up to until he rolled over on top of me and muttered, 'Make a bad boy out of me!'

"Honestly I was totally bewildered. I didn't mind him kissing me because his stubble was gently scratchy but his hands wandered everywhere, and I couldn't keep up with them. He opened my shirt in about six seconds and it took me a whole five minutes to fight him off and extract the hand. He was really surprised that I hadn't responded ardently to such a thrusting approach. Personally it felt like a cavalry charge. Anyway I explained that I wasn't quite prepared for such a start to the evening, and though he seemed like a genuine enough young man, he had perhaps overestimated my potential.

"I had to say something—he looked at me as if I were a frigid spinster. So I changed the subject and asked him if I could change the tape on his tape player because there was a girl singing who sounded as if she were holding her nose and singing underwater. I looked through the tape to find something that didn't suggest sex, but the whole car was rigged like a passion wagon. Whatever it was I put on, he sang along to it while we wrestled. He had a flat voice and kept getting the words wrong. So I told him I had to go to the loo desperately and he would have to take me to The Fisherman's Inn, a couple of miles along the bay. He wasn't going to take me, he kept saying, "You'd rather stay here with me," and laughing the way Dracula would before he sucks the blood out of a virgin. I insisted, and said that if he didn't I would leave a puddle on the furry red, white and blue car seat right on top of the Union Jack motif I was sitting on. So he drove us to the inn and ungraciously bought me a Guinness, which I felt I deserved. There was a condom machine in the ladies loo. It was disgusting. Derek then stroked my leg under the table and commented in undertones that everyone else looked like a Fenian—which he pronounced like Kenyan—their eyes were too close together, he said. I said I had to get home at 11 on the dot on a Sunday night as my mother was very strict about things like that. He had the car parked at the front door and was launching into another bit of passion when someone switched on the porch light. I think it was mummy to see if I was snogging like a normal girl. I said, 'Oh that will be my mother coming to check you out,' and he dropped me as if I had said I had BO and it was contagious. So I escaped intact."

She paused for breath.

"Do all men go on like that?"

Dear Richard,

What manner of letter was the last you posted me? Inkstained hieroglyphics I expect, yes, but the pervasive aroma of sheep from the paper leads me to deduce that you composed it in an outhouse with hands unwashed. Have your ewes begun lambing? Ours have barely finished conceiving in this isolated Ulster icecap.

And Richard, really, I know academic aspirations dissolve from you on leaving the Pale but your handwriting must be illegible to anyone but me— after all didn't I spend as much time deciphering your lecture notes for you as I did sorting through the looped lettering of my own? I believe we two hold the honour of never having been asked twice for the loan of notes in the Ag faculty.

I am trotting briskly through Siegfried Sassoon's Memoirs of a Fox-Hunting Man *and it put me in the mood to ride. The Ag college stables have three* quite uninspiring nags and one flighty thoroughbred who belongs to a food science student. The three nags—carrying three quiet and uninspiring riders—accompanied Ginger and me on a hack on Wednesday last. Wednesday is the sports and recreation day at Ag college the way it is at school. The three nags broke into shambling heavy canters as we passed a football match. I had been admiring the physique of one of the opposition and didn't notice them taking off. Ginger panicked as she thought they were getting away without her and she wasn't interested in any footballer's legs. She took off after them with the true grit of a war-horse, except that her rider, me, wasn't controlling her.

Bolting horses don't scare me because I reckon they have to stop sometime, so I sat tight and enjoyed the speed while Ginger raced to catch up with the trailing nags. It was too nice a day to think about Ginger breaking her knees on the nearby road and me being scraped off a lorry and being posted home in a plastic bag.

She straddled a low fence from the sports field into an overgrown unused lane, stopped dead and looked round her for a bit. We jumped back out to encounter three frantic and slightly hysterical riders. They thought I was dead or worse—can't think *what worse might be.*

I am most disappointed to miss the Ag ball this year and I'm sure you regret that there will not be a repeat performance of last year's spectacle! I have an invitation to Queen's Psychology ball and it is unfortunate that it is on the same evening. I hope you misbehave outrageously and cause major scandal.

Speaking of scandal, it seems Daisy took to heart my chats on "these are the days to remember for they will not last forever" and has been misbehaving magnificently, to the delight of the Ag faculty. She says the first day she came back after Christmas wearing her checked mini-skirt comments varied from: "Was it Oxfam, or did your mother make it?" to "I bet she is only wearing it for a dare."

After she shifted Brendan Ó Muircheartaigh, the esteemed auditor of Ag Soc, at the pre-ball disco a poster appeared on the glass-fronted notice board in the Ag block:

"Witnesses to Daisy Gordon's Classic Shifting Techniques, Lansdowne, Thursday night," with about 40 signatures. She had to break into the notice board with the porter's screwdriver to retrieve it. Brendan is taking her to the ball; it looks as if romance is blossoming again for D and Charlie has been swept well under the carpet. She has offered

*to keep an eye on you throughout the evening but
I should think Brendan will keep her occupied and
I suspect Elisabeth will have you on a tight rein.*

"Don't let her Richard!!"

*I intend to have a wonderful evening with my
Queen's psychologist though he drinks Malibu and
pineapple and may appear in lemon bow-tie and
matching socks.*

*No matter—a ball is what you make it, and
this one may be even better than an Ag ball. Give
my love to Mick and Elisabeth, and, Richard, don't
spank Elisabeth if she comes on strong: she is not
a female spider.*

I signed myself, *Love, Helen*, which I never did with
Richard because it embarrassed him. But I had had a
premonition of change as I wrote his letter and I
sensed that after 25 Jan, the night of our twin balls,
something was going to change for ever.

Maurice, my psychologist, wore pink to com-
plement my Scarlett dress and became sozzled on
three Malibu and pineapple. After he dozed off, his
elbow in an overflowing ashtray, I took off to the loo
to plot my fortuitous escape...

Hugh Stewart was standing in the foyer of the
hotel. My heart kicked like an ostrich and I stopped
mid-stride. In slow motion he looked up at me and

our eyes locked and I couldn't move. He came over.

"Wicked lady," he smiled, and I swallowed.

"I thought you were a student of life." It was the first thing that popped into my head. He laughed. "I am," he said. "But I am also doing a Master's degree." I wasn't listening to him just looking at him but I heard him explain something about getting bored with his job and returning to Queen's for some further education.

Why did my heart flip like that when he smiled? Was it because I had fancied him for years and had shifted him twice? And if I had anything to do with it I was going to shift him again? Did he even realise how attractive he was when he looked deep into my eyes and laughed like that?

"I assume you are here with a date?" he raised one eyebrow and I was glad I had worn the Scarlett dress.

"My date is in a drunken slumber and, if there is a God in heaven, he will remain as such for 100 years. You?"

I was dying to know if he had a girlfriend stashed away.

"My girlfriend," he waved a hand as if to banish all thought of her, "is a lady."

We danced together, sat out together, chatted, danced again. I was convinced I was in love by the end of the evening.

I felt nothing when I heard that Richard had shifted Elisabeth—remoteness, as if it had happened many years ago and to different people. I knew Richard had had many women but he usually kept his conquests discreet and to my knowledge never mixed business with pleasure. Daisy said Elisabeth had the three B's, brains, breeding and beauty. As such, she and Richard were perfect for each other.

Dear Richard,

Don't you love the spring? Wordsworth would have a field-day among the daffodils in our orchard, and when I walked up to the milking parlour this morning the sun was peeping through a frosty mist and the paddocks were pink-stained. Instantly I thought of Browning's "Pippa's Song,"—you know: "God's in his Heaven; all's right with the world."

Lee is visiting and the experience is both educational and enjoyable. As he is your typical American, larger than life, daddy took an instant dislike to him although they are relatively related. He stays in Dublin with Laura ("he sleeps on the sofa, mummy") and as far as I know, she packs him off to pound Guinness with the rougher elements in class when she has to study. I visited them last weekend. Lee claims to be an awesome cook and entertains Laura from the kitchen—you know she can't boil water. She says she entertains him with her stimulating conversation and their expounding of cultural differences. I'll say no more except that I slept on the sofa and it was too short for me. Daisy is giving no secrets away but I suspect Laura pays her to sleep on the sofa in the living room when Elisabeth is in her own bed.

Although our religion doesn't demand it, are you attempting any Lenten sacrifice this year? Do you remember last year I tried to stop swearing and had a swear-box into which I deposited silver coins when I let myself down? And how magnificent I was for a week until my chemistry experiment boiled over and I burnt my fingers lifting it away from the heat. "Damnation," I yelped and dropped the beaker, and it smashed on the floor (two days' work splattered at my feet). And then I remembered that I had given up swearing. "Bloody bloody hell," I said to you, "I swore."

It is easier this year because Sylvia and I are encouraging each other. We forfeited the swear-box idea as Sylvia would require a bank overdraft if she contributed every time she said a bad word. I consider myself almost virtuous in comparison.

I suggested to Laura that she give up Lee but she laughed pityingly at me. It doesn't matter how often Mick has to carry him home from the bar—he can't *match the Irish boys—she is totally besotted by her "house-boy" and his visit threatens to stretch into the summer and beyond. It seems he jacked in his illustrious restaurant career to come to Ireland. It appears too that Mick and he have become really friendly, and Mick doesn't mind a bit that Laura threw him over for a Yank. They must have had a purely superficial relationship after all.*

CHAPTER ELEVEN

My new love interest in Hugh waxed rather than waned after our first few evenings of exploration and discovery. He possessed all the characteristics I demanded in my Mr Wonderful and seemed to possess a few that I hadn't taken into consideration before. It struck me that he had never tipped a car seat in his life. When I asked him as much he laughed—and my heart did its usual double-twisting-back somersault—and said he had never owned a car to try it. He did however possess a racing bicycle and I found it an eccentric turn-on to be conveyed around Belfast on his crossbar. Soon I was visiting him every weekend though he did suggest that he take the bus to Derryrose and stay there.

"No!" It sounded like a pistol shot, and he stepped back a little insulted.

"No," I croaked, "You can't possibly come to Derryrose. It isn't safe. My mother is hyperactive and has Empty Nest syndrome, and my father doesn't talk to strangers. And if you are male and under thirty he may use you for target practice—as he did with

Ian."

It was essential that Hugh didn't get near my house because he was much too special to submit to our special Derryrose brand of madness. In fact I was so keen on him I had cut back on the other men dramatically. I was almost faithful.

There was just the mountain man, Harold, that I had the odd romp in the hayshed with at Ag college, and the communications student, Mervin, with whom I discussed the finer points of Receiver/Response. He was kinda cute. And what with visiting Hugh almost every weekend I had no time to notch my bedpost with anyone else.

I suppose everything worked out OK because everyone else seemed to be studying—except me. Hugh said I released the monotony and depression of his Master's course. Lee, it appeared, was carrying Laura through her pre-finals trauma—if she had any, which I doubt. His devotion was touching and Daisy had observed him ironing her shirt one morning as she rushed out for a nine o'clock lecture.

Daddy had taken a dislike to him, though, and when I suggested that he was devoted to Laura, he simply snorted and said: "That hoodlum is trespassing on the hospitality of my daughter. Laura is too kind and too soft-hearted to turn him out!"

It was a good job he never suspected what the

relationship really was or he would have taken a posse to Dublin—all armed with shotguns—to defend his eldest's honour, and retrieve her from the Hooded Claw in the form of his colonial relative. As it was he was simply Not Welcome at Derryrose.

As the bright yellow days of spring lengthened into a cloudless May I ceased writing to Richard completely. His replies had become mechanical responses and the tone of his letters suggested indifference. Hurt pride compelled me to stop corresponding because though I was fully and satisfyingly occupied with Hugh my happiness wasn't entirely unblemished. A black cloud with "Richard" imprinted on it loomed in the back of my mind though I would have cut my tongue out faster than admit it.

Laura got a Two-One degree, which considering her extra-curricular activities and her room-mate was exceptional. Daddy claimed to care nothing for her academic success but I overheard him telling the Ministry man who had come to supervise the sheep dipping.

Aided and abetted by Hugh, I instructed my parents on what was expected of them on Graduation Day. Daddy refused point-blank to treat Laura to dinner in a restaurant of her choice. Once, years ago he had found a feather in a chicken burger he had bought in a chip shop and from thenceforth had refused to sacrifice his valuable health to the catering trade. Laura threatened to throw the first wobbly of her career—for she was even-tempered as a rule. While he remained inflexible, it remained for Lee, of all people, to pour oil on the troubled waters. He was a qualified chef and when mummy and daddy were observing the conferring of their daughter's degree he would be cooking them lunch in the flat they were sharing in Dublin. Laura told mummy that she was working at the perfume counter in one of the large department stores on Grafton Street and her wages were too impressive for her to jack it all in and return to obscurity at Derryrose. I don't think mummy believed this—for she had streetwise friends even if she had no opportunity to be streetwise herself. But daddy believed her and that was all that mattered.

"That slum," said daddy, "My digestion will suffer irrevocably if I am subjected to the food cooked by that villain in Laura's ghetto flat."

Mummy dealt with daddy's rebellious mutterings in her own way, and daddy resigned himself to years off his life. I can't think why he considered Lee's cooking could be in any way inferior to mummy's. She had baked a cake for Jennifer's eighteenth birthday but had become so absorbed in *A Damsel Betrayed* that she had left what had promised to be a Victoria sponge in the oven for an hour and a half. Daddy had heroically attempted the remains because he was convinced that if he didn't give the appearance of enjoying such contributions she might stop completely. Only *he* thought this a tragedy.

Wonderful wonderful Hugh invited me to meet his parents at his graduation lunch which though I felt it a daunting proposition I agreed to. He had been offered his Doctor's degree, and the path of fortune lay shining and inviting before him. I was secretly flattered that he wanted to share it with me. Best of all was that he preserved his nonchalant humour in the face of such accolades and still took me joy-riding on the crossbar of his bicycle.

"You are a lucky, lucky girl," I informed my reflection the night before his graduation. Because Laura didn't graduate until later in the summer I was to act as scout and discover how parents were supposed to behave and dress on these ostentatious occasions. I don't know why I bothered because we knew that daddy would make an exhibition of himself as he always did, and mummy would flirt with any attractive man she saw, regardless of his age, married status, and daddy's restraining eye.

Hugh's parents appeared normal enough, until, after a glass of dull sweet wine, his mother piped up:

"I suppose Hugh has told you his middle name?"

She had a disarming habit of leaning really close to you when she spoke and I felt suffocated in the half bottle of perfume she had poured over herself.

"No he hasn't," I said sweetly, attempting to untangle myself from her and catching Hugh's eye. I had a wild desire to laugh. I had privately constructed the W to represent many things including wonderful, and wonderful, and wonderful again. But no.

"It's Winston." Hugh's mother giggled conspiratorially and I allowed myself a weak smile. Hugh was stroking my calf under the table with his foot and I wasn't sure if I could take the pressure much longer.

His father thought the issue of Hugh's middle name as big a joke as his mother because, having restrained himself manfully up to that point, he boomed—and he had a very loud, sergeant-major type of voice— "He looked just like Churchill in his cradle."

They both laughed and Hugh caught my eye and we both laughed too, though, of course, they never suspected that we were laughing at them and not with them. And to think that I had worried that my parents were odd! Hugh could visit Derryrose anytime: he would fit in perfectly the way Richard couldn't.

Dammit, Richard had just popped into my head, trying to spoil my fun. He had gone to spend the summer in England with cousins, Daisy had said. She had seen him in UCD the day he had been there for his practical year exam. He sent me one postcard from Kent, with a picture of a fox on it and "Sun isn't as hot here, sky isn't as blue." scrawled on the back. From it I deduced that he preferred Ireland and maliciously hoped he had to endure England all summer. I thought I had successfully transcribed the initial feelings of hurt and rejection into active dislike. Active because I had to keep working on the dislike and convincing myself I was better off without him.

Laura's graduation passed without incident until, over lunch, mummy asked her what she intended doing with herself now she had graduated so impressively.

"You can't sell perfume all your life," she said, attacking Lee's Pork Deerstalker with the gluttonous appetite she reserved for really good cooking. She always excused her own appalling cookery by claiming that if she fed us, her daughters, too well we would be fat and get no clothes to fit us and no man to marry us. She still had the smallest waist I have ever seen.

"I'm going to America to live with Lee," and mummy choked on her flambéed carrots. Daddy who still hadn't caught on exclaimed, "But, Laura, people will start to think you are living in sin with him."

Lee had been promoted from non-existent to

"him": daddy also appreciated good food.

"Well sir," said Lee, opening his mouth and stepping straight in, "Well sir, we have talked of marriage, but Laura and I think there is no point rushing into anything. Laura isn't certain that she wants to remain permanently in the States yet."

Things got physical then with daddy grabbing Lee by the throat and demanding to know just what he had been doing to his daughter—as if Laura had been the Virgin Mary, and a vessel of celestial purity, to be preserved sacred and chaste.

Lee was about six inches taller than daddy, and a lot heavier, but he was rather taken aback, as a Rottweiler would be if attacked by a terrier. Mummy, it seems, left her pork long enough to drag daddy off Lee (who was helplessly turning blue—he could hardly attack his prospective father-in-law with a fork). Laura flung herself on Lee and defiantly informed daddy that she was going to live with Lee and that was that and if he didn't start behaving she would go to America and never come back.

This calmed daddy sufficiently for him to consider the situation logically. As Laura was the Orange-woman among his daughters, he knew he would be a sorry boy to allow her to escape. So, with an air of martyred righteousness, he shook Lee's hand and swallowing audibly suggested they spend some time at Derryrose before making any hasty decisions. Then they finished the pork—no shock could be so great that daddy couldn't eat—and by the time they were leaving Dublin mummy had talked him into accepting an American son-in-law.

"And he is such a wonderful cook," said mummy.

Brendan Ó Muircheartaigh's family had a summer house in Kerry and he gave Daisy the keys after her exams and told her to "away and enjoy yourself." He had got a job with the Scottish Milk Marketing Board, so she took Sarah, Jennifer and me for company.

As we rattled down to Tralee on the train I gazed out of the carriage window and was convinced there were daffodils growing in the fields. Certainly Ireland was a mystical and unpredictable country but daffodils in June was asking a bit much. I commented as much to Daisy who looked vague and said she believed the flowers to be flaggers, the yellow Iris species that inhabited land subjected to Artesian seepage. Jennifer and Sarah assumed admiring expressions. I decided that agricultural college had ruined any intelligence I had ever possessed.

Tralee Railway Station Information Office informed us that there was no bus service to Cahirdaniel village, and when the girl mentioned that it was sixty miles away, I sensed Sarah crumble beside me. It had been a tough job to prise her away from Ian for a week and upset in these preliminary stages threatened to break her completely.

"We'll hitch—" I enthused, "—have a real adventure."

"Be raped and pillaged, our purity ravaged and our cigarettes stolen more like," said Jennifer, who cheered up remarkably after the best glass of Guinness she had ever had. Jennifer wasn't intending to become an Ag student but if the need arose she could pass herself magnificently. Even Sarah had a glass though it was with initial trepidation. Every time the pub door swung open she glanced up guiltily to ensure it was neither Ian nor Reverend Robinson, both of whom preached incessantly on the evils of drink. Even our assurances that Ian was probably painting the kerbstone red white and blue in anticipation of the Twelfth didn't console her. He hadn't wanted her in this land of heretics at all, she said, but he was no match for the three of us, and we overruled his pompous and bigoted suggestions. Having previously pitied him, I now thought him an insufferable cad.

We hitched in couples, Jennifer and I gave Daisy and Sarah a head-start of the drinking time for another glass of stout; then we trudged after them.

Getting lifts in Kerry is great fun. The locals are very friendly and delighted to give foreigners lifts. A foreigner is anybody who wasn't born in Kerry. One old man driving a dilapidated Morris Minor said he was only going as far as Cahersiveen, but he drove us on to Waterville as he claimed that the scenery was more breathtaking along the less used road. Jennifer prodded me to indicate that she considered this the moment when he would produce a ripsaw from under the car seat, with which to dismember us. But he was a decent man, and if only I had understood even one sentence of his particular dialect, the lift couldn't have been more enjoyable.

Jennifer, as a child, had been flashed at by a car-driver and was consequently very cautious about lift-taking. She dragged me on in Waterville when she discovered me making eyes at a huge Scandinavian posing on the bonnet of a Saab car. When the Scandinavian and two of his equally blond mates followed us up the road in their ancient Saab she insisted I turn my face to the hedge and ignore them.

"I could possibly endure being raped and pillaged by an Irishman but certainly not by a foreigner."

Daisy and Sarah weren't in the pub-shop in Cahirdaniel when we eventually reached there, but they turned up two glasses of Guinness later with Arthur, a soft drinks salesman, in tow. Arthur had lifted them in Cahersiveen in his yellow Hiace van and they had accompanied him to Valentia Island on the way to Cahirdaniel, while Arthur dropped off crates of alcohol-free lager. Jennifer and I exchanged glances that said, "If Arthur, the soft drinks salesman, thinks he is staying tonight with us, he can think again."

However Arthur left after one glass of lemonade and a filthy joke that embarrassed Sarah and made Jennifer laugh.

Brendan's summer house was light and airy and very bright and we advised Daisy to keep well in with the Ó Muircheartaighs as they must be rolling in money. Not having any money ourselves solvency impressed us as nothing else did.

"Pity they are Catholic," said Sarah but Jennifer threw a shoe at her to shut her up. You could hear Ian speak through her constantly.

There was tremendous heat the week we stayed in Cahirdaniel, and we all burned alarmingly—except Sarah, who tanned immediately—and the pub-shop never did such a roaring trade in brown vinegar before or again. We used brown vinegar to cool the burning. Daddy never allowed us to use cream as he said it clogged the pores. Once, the year he was married, he had "caught" sunstroke bringing in hay, and now he never ventured outdoors without his burnt sunhat, and a long-sleeved shirt. Mummy, on the other hand, from whom Sarah had inherited the tanning skin, spent hot days in a skimpy bikini, which embarrassed daddy, and duped our neighbours into thinking she had been on holiday. Cahirdaniel is not the place to visit if you want a raunchy holiday. In fact apart from the Scandinavian rapists in the Saab we met no men under the age of fifty. This was great for Sarah who could pine convincingly for Ian but the rest of us had been counting on a bit of interaction with the natives. My rucksack would have weighed less than half what it did if I had realised that there was no chance of a big night out, and that I was to spend my days doing *The Irish Times* crosswords in a pile of newspapers I had discovered in the woodbox beside the fire.

Once I had resigned myself to a week of celibacy I had a great time, what with the view, the heat and the humungous bottle of wine Brendan had considerately left for us. I rather fancied Cahirdaniel for a honeymoon, especially if it rained all the time and my husband and I had to spend the entire time in bed.

Daisy took a lot of scenery photographs which she later framed as her Kerry collection. But for the fact that her camera was bought for £10 in the Argos catalogue she could have been a formidable photographer—she could make a clump of foxgloves in an empty field appear breathtakingly artistic.

I stuck to puerile snapshots of Jennifer stuffing her face with crab, Sarah swaddling a guilty glass of Guinness and Daisy lying prostrate in the hot sand "listening to the music of the sea." On the last evening we cooked dinner between us and discussed sex, love and beauty.

Daisy contributed a bag of raspberries she had picked along the hedges during a photographic expedition and a bottle of milk that was lying in a convenient ditch. She said (with a wink at me) that though Brendan was both decisive and rich he was a Catholic—Sarah nodded her approval—his fingers were short and stubby, and he laughed at her flower pressing. Sarah whose offering was a bag of potatoes—like daddy she didn't think a meal was complete without potatoes—said that she considered Ian almost perfect. We, naturally, pounced on the *almost* and she finally admitted that he sometimes lorded it over her because he had money while we didn't.

"Pahh," said Jennifer rudely, "He is a nouveau riche upstart Sarah. He isn't rich: he just has money."

It wasn't only Jennifer who was affronted. I was cross too and Daisy said, "Gentlemen never wear bracelets, Sarah," and poor old Sarah got all hot and bothered and nearly cried.

Then Jennifer chirped up, "Tell us this, Sarah, and tell us no more: are you and Ian at it?"

Sarah, all defences smashed, muttered "No," Ian respected her too much and praised virtue in a woman above all else. Her face was, well, disappointed almost.

Jennifer didn't have a boyfriend so she consented to give us a description of her ideal man. Foodwise she gave us some bags of salt and vinegar crisps, and a big bunch of wild rhododendron, which looked pretty if not edible.

Jennifer's man had brown curly hair and grey eyes. He was an astronaut and would be away in space a lot so he didn't suffocate her. When he came home they would have mighty crack and when he was away she would never wash. She was a dirty brute by nature.

I supplied the party with two packets of cream of chicken soup and told them how Hugh had kissed the top of my head during our farewell shift and warned me to leave his Walkman behind if I went swimming in case I drowned, as it had cost him a lot of money. I wasn't sure if I adored this type of behaviour or if it frustrated me.

"I detect," said Daisy, in a sing-song voice, "that if there was no shadow of Richard Knight obscuring your vision, my dear, the noble Hugh would be the man for you."

She glanced at Jennifer and Sarah. "Because though she doesn't want to realise it," she said to them, "Hugh is only a substitute for Richard."

I told her to shut up because hard truth is difficult to swallow with salt and vinegar crisps.

CHAPTER TWELVE

My parents emphatically implored Laura to change her mind and her boyfriend but of course she paid no heed and planned to fly to New Jersey with Lee in August. She was a model daughter the few weeks she and Lee stayed at Derryrose and even attended the Twelfth with daddy though it rained the entire day and she caught a chill from her soaking. Only mummy didn't mind the rain as it gave her the opportunity to show off her new mauve mackintosh which matched her purple trousers and purple and white striped shirt—purple for passion she said. She even had a purple stripe on her sports shoes. I had felt a flutter of patriotism on the Eleventh night, watching Lee hoisting our Union Jack on to the roof of the cow byre, and almost made up my mind to go too. But the rain and the forlorn saturated flag disheartened me on the Twelfth morning and I stayed most of the day in bed reading *Love in a Cold Climate* instead.

Daisy and I went out on the Twelfth night and shifted two Republican sympathisers from Toomebridge. Daddy calls the village Toomestone because so many people were shot there. Hugh had gone to Israel for two months to pick fruit before starting his PhD, or I might have behaved myself. I suppose I could have gone with him but,

1. I was adverse to hard labour;
2. My skin was too fair;
3. I wanted to be there when Laura left.

He sent me postcards in code. They contained no highbrow content but they entertained me immensely and baffled the postman and my family, neither of whom were above reading correspondence that wasn't for them.

We all cried at the airport when Laura and Lee left. Laura didn't cry. She was radiant and it showed. Love, I reasoned, must be stupid as well as blind.

I was delighted when Jennifer obtained a monotonous four A's in her A Levels and chose to study veterinary science in Dublin. Everyone was surprised by this burst of hitherto concealed genius in the youngest Gordon, except the lady herself, who had as high an opinion of her brainpower as she had of her looks.

"You must move in with me," I offered, not because I thought she would be a model flat-mate, but because she was my little sister and didn't know anyone in Dublin. I knew already that she would be unbearable to live with.

Jennifer said that she did not wish to live with me.

"And be referred to as 'Helen's little sister' constantly? No way."

But the horror stories I told her of the hostel Laura and I had endured in our first year soon changed her mind.

"It wouldn't be the food," she conceded, "because, God knows, our mother will never be successful in the kitchen—" (We had had Spaghetti Bolognese the day before with daddy demanding potatoes.) "—it's the restriction. The Warden sounds worse than a nun."

I was not pleased when Daisy suggested Elisabeth as the third person for the flat. In truth I was jealous of the fabled Elisabeth, whom I had never met, because Richard had preferred her to me.

"You are being silly Helen." Daisy was quite severe with me. "Richard Knight only shifted her once and they were both a bit tipsy at the time. Elisabeth admits quite freely that it was a silly thing to do. There is absolutely nothing between them. I think you are a fool not to move in with her because I think you will both really like each other."

By the end of Daisy's first fortnight at agricultural college she had been labelled "Lazy Daisy" which she said she didn't deserve because she made a genuine effort to work though there seemed to be countless distractions. I thought she meant the food science students but by November she had ditched Brendan and acquired a small fat boy.

"It's wrong to assume," she wrote, "that the small fats are our intellectual inferiors, they are simply on a different plane of intelligence." She said she really fancied Willy and he was teaching her to play snooker. Daddy was delighted because it was the first Ulster boyfriend Daisy had ever dated and his father was even an Orangeman.

Regardless of Daisy's prophecy I was prepared to dislike Elisabeth intensely right up to the moment we met. Daisy may have bestowed on her brains, beauty and breeding but the Elisabeth of my imagination had the face of a horse, and heavy hockey-players' thighs. She would wear a husky jacket, have broken veins in her cheeks and thin hair. She would reek of old money and affluence. I would loathe her.

The girl curled up on the sofa in the Palmerston Road sitting room was painting her nails and eating a box of chocolates. When she saw me, rucksacked and parched she said, "Oh, my dear, take that bag off your back and have a chocolate. You can have whatever one you want except the caramel. They are simply my favourite favourites."

I liked her immediately. Elisabeth, like the princess

in all fairy tales, had long golden hair and china-doll blue eyes. She was so pretty that if I had been Richard I would have shifted her too.

"That wine in the bedroom," she said, about ten minutes after we had met. "It smells of silage effluent. What is it?"

"Elderberry," I replied amused. Silage effluent indeed!

"Does it taste like silage effluent?" Eyes wide with innocence.

So we drank the bottle of elderberry wine to decide, then we drank another to be sure. And as the potency of homemade wine is always vastly underrated, we were both a little merry by the end of the second bottle.

"Oh Helen," said Elisabeth faintly, "I feel most peculiar." She giggled deliciously. "Isn't it wonderful to be a silly girl, and not be expected to have a brain? Brains make me so nervous. At Trinity we have them walking round, huge tedious brains encased in high foreheads behind horn-rimmed spectacles. And they look at me with my one brain cell and they thank God that I don't have two or I would be dangerous. Sweet thing," she laughed, "I know that you agree with me because Richard told me so."

She, my rival, included Richard's name so casually into the conversation, it was as if the name meant nothing to her. My heart bounded and thumped against my ribcage alarmingly.

"Richard?" I said in a voice of melodious falseness, "What nonsense was he spouting?"

"Nonsense." More laughter. "Yes it is nonsense he speaks. Chivalrous Victorian strait-laced nonsense. It isn't his fault, Helen; his family haven't evolved since the famine or the partition or Cromwell, I haven't decided which. His father still wears collar studs, and you know there isn't a bit of heat in his house."

I didn't think it was the time to reveal that Derryrose had two radiators, neither of which worked, and that the temperature of my bedroom was normally lower than that of the fridge. Mummy was a fresh-air freak and went around opening windows. Daddy followed in her wake shutting them. When she nailed open the kitchen windows he wore his overcoat indoors in silent protest.

"Richard says you are a pineapple tart," said Elisabeth suddenly.

"A what?"

"Oh I wish I was a pineapple tart," she added wistfully.

"What," I asked, "is a pineapple tart?"

"A pineapple tart is the highest form of compliment any woman can be given," explained Elisabeth solemnly, tipping the wine bottle upside down to make sure there was no silage effluent left in it and resigning herself to another chocolate.

"He disapproves entirely of me," I insisted. "He says I am a loose woman because I paint my face."

"No no, darling, he worships you. Flirtatious yet womanly, wanton and warm, you are the woman he admires, sweet as pineapple. Of course you scare him, so he is odiously badly behaved with you. I wish I could be a pineapple tart but Richard says I'm not because I only love myself. He's right of course."

She laughed delightfully, more silver bells.

"I am frivolous and trivial and silly."

"But you and Richard," I persisted. "You and Richard..."

"Darling," she stopped laughing and turned her china-blue eyes on me. "Darling you don't really think that we are courting?"

Courting was very quaint, very Richard.

"You shifted," I defended myself. She was my rival, yet she could be my friend; I had to know.

"Silly moo," she smiled. "We exchanged a few tipsy kisses. He isn't my cup of tea at all. Hides his sex appeal, too formal, too W B Yeats, above all that. I like a man with his feet on the ground and his mind on me. Richard Knight is a one-woman man and I am not that woman."

I wondered if I was that woman.

Elisabeth's thoughts tripped on like a child running down a path, chasing butterflies.

"I love Daisy," she said. "I love her sense of style. We spent so many hours in charity shops last year it was appalling. Daisy and I made this dress from a curtain."

She waited for my approval, a pretty child showing off her pretty dress. The dress was very Daisy, a drop waist gold satin creation. I could imagine Elisabeth dressed in a fertiliser bag looking like The Lady of Shallott or Rapunzel letting down her golden hair—but for whom? Not Richard, of that I am sure. She was right. Richard wasn't her cup of tea. Friendship and relief welled inside me, twin souls.

I never heard anyone refer to Jennifer as "Helen's little sister," possibly because she was taller than me, and they knew she would have poked their eyes out if they had. It was just as well Elisabeth and I were sharing a room and she had one of her own because she kept rather erratic hours and claimed that the work wasn't intense enough to disrupt her socialising. Her vet friends were rather wild. One particular character called herself Astra, though I knew her name to be Maeve, and had peroxide-blonde hair and a black leather mini-skirt. Having met her, Elisabeth suggested that she must appear a little incongruous in the vet faculty. To Elisabeth, women vets were mountainous heifers who beat up bullocks before breakfast.

"She looks no dafter than Daisy sticking her hand up a cow's bum," Jennifer had shrugged and the matter closed.

Jennifer disliked Charlie—now house surgeon at the vet college—on sight.

"How could Daisy bear him?" she asked me. "He just sauntered over to me the first time he saw me, looked me up and down and drawled, 'Well unless I am very much mistaken, you are Daisy Gordon's sister.'"

Obviously this had maddened Jennifer who loathes to be compared with any of us. But what could she expect, being the youngest?

"And what did you say?" I asked her—I still liked Charlie, B category and all. He reminded me of the happier days when Richard and I were friends.

"I said and I imitated that superior drawl of his, I said, 'And unless I am very much mistaken you must be that toffee-nosed twit Daisy shifted while she was having an identity crisis.'"

It seems that they glared at each other and stomped off in different directions.

Daisy laughed when I recounted the incident to her at Hallowe'en. She had cried long and hard over Charlie but had never looked back since.

"You know," she explained, "I thought I had met my Prince Charming when Charlie said 'Buy the Alpen: it's on special offer this week.' My heart flipped the way Cinderella's did when the slipper fitted. And he was such a masterful prince. Far too masterful for me. So that's why there was no story-book ending. I brainwashed myself into believing that his over-bearing was protectiveness, and I wasn't strong enough for him. Anyway, he always thought that classical music should be confined to television commercials, and that the Romantic poets were raving homosexuals."

She pouted. She practised the pout constantly in her room at Ag college when she was sent to study. It was perfect now.

"Jennifer and Charlie would be a very interesting combination you know," she added, not really looking at me. "They are realists, both brilliantly intelligent. Think of the IQ of the kids they would produce."

Brave words I thought. I wouldn't have fancied the first love of my life getting intimate with one of my sisters.

"How's Richard?" Her voice cut gently into my thoughts. I hated the way Daisy brought up the subject of Richard. It disarmed me and made me nervous. Anyway, there was nothing to tell. I had convinced myself that what ever notion I had had of him had been just that, a notion. I was wise enough to know that we couldn't have continued to amble along as friends for ever while I harboured passionate intentions. But I had hoped to recapture at least a little of our past understanding. As it stood, he was barely civil to me, it was only his Victorian code of conduct that resulted in his saying "Good Morning" at all. Anyway, Hugh was a much easier person to go out with and, if I didn't love him, I certainly liked him better than anyone else I knew, Richard included.

"Still in love with him," Daisy mused, watching my face, "And still trying not to be."

I changed the subject.

"I really like Elisabeth," I said, "She is awfully pretty."

Daisy laughed. "She wrote to me last week," she said by way of explanation. "Do you know what she said? She said, 'I really like Helen, she is awfully pretty.' I suppose you have a mutual admiration society in Palmerston Road."

Richard and I had one blazing encounter before Christmas at a twenty-first-birthday party we had been invited to. Up until the night of the party we had continued to pretend that we were still friends but he had started to get mad with me over the most trivial things. "He told me I embarrassed him," I stormed one evening at tea. "Richard Knight said I was an embarrassment."

Elisabeth had been sympathetic.

"What embarrassed him?" she asked, peeling her fifth potato. For such a frail-looking princess, she could pack away her potatoes.

"I said that Hugh was coming down for the weekend when we were at lunch. You know yourself that Hugh comes down nearly every weekend."

She winked at me. "Yes I know." She thought Hugh was very attractive. "Your intended" she called him.

"And Mick was having lunch with us and he said something coarse, you know about Hugh being here—nudge, nudge, wink wink—that sort of thing, and I laughed and Richard almost ate me when Mick left. He said I was common and an embarrassment and if I insisted on conducting my love-affairs here in Dublin, would I kindly not discuss them in his vicinity."

"He's jealous," said Elisabeth licking her fingers and looking round the kitchen for something else to eat.

"But he's not," I scowled. "Because I have always had love-affairs since I have known him and he never cared before."

"Well I think he is jealous of your intended," said Elisabeth, firmly, hacking at a date-and-walnut loaf I had brought down from home. "Think how suitable

Hugh is, Helen, and how handsome. He outshines Richard."

Hugh and Richard had met and were pleasant to each other. In fact Richard had been almost friendly. Hugh spent his weekends in Dublin as he considered it more aesthetically conducive to courting than Belfast. Instead of travelling on his crossbar now I sat on Emily's handlebars and he pedalled when we wanted to go anywhere.

"If Richard was that keen on me," I said, "he would do something about it."

Richard asked me to dance at the party. I felt that he didn't really want to because his shoulders were stiff and he didn't speak. He whirled me round as if dancing were a military exercise, and not a particularly pleasant one at that.

I felt all sentimental (probably I had drunk too much port) and touched his cheek timidly: "Richard," I said, "let's be friends."

Checked emotion erupted through his blank features and he dragged me off the dance floor and out to the foyer of the hall. The imprint of his fingers left red marks on my arm but I was too astounded by his behaviour to say anything. Richard Knight simply didn't drag women off dance floors.

"You slut, you mindless self-pleasing slut, prancing about in that tight dress teasing every man who looks at you using them and throwing them away. You make me sick."

I didn't hear the rest of the tirade. There was a pounding in my ears and stars danced in front of my eyes. I was gobsmacked.

Though my hand itched to come in contact with the face that was abusing me I resisted and instead said, "I was unaware how you felt, Richard," freezing voice, burning cheeks. My hands were trembling but of course he couldn't see that, the palms bleeding where I had dug my nails into them.

"I thought we had agreed that my behaviour was none of your business. I can do what ever I want, so mind your own business."

I had started with remarkable constraint but by the time I was blurting out "mind your own business" I was aware that I was screaming. Richard always brought out the fishwife in me.

"It is my business!" He was screaming too—Richard who had for years preached that, "A public display of emotion is an embarrassing and degrading performance."

"Of course it's my business."

He didn't say, "It's my business because I am in love with you," but the words unspoken hung like heavy perfume between us.

A man like Richard, in love, and not wanting to

be, and trying to hide it—unsuccessfully—acts like a fool, and his shouting at me was ridiculous behaviour.

Of course it was, except that I couldn't see it because I was in love with him, and didn't want to be, and was hiding it—more successfully.

He was still gripping my arm and I snapped, "Take your hands off me," and spun round to leave him.

Maliciously he muttered, "You are a silly woman."

Hugh could see that I was flustered when I rejoined him, having gone outdoors to kick a few car wheels to calm down. He raised one eyebrow enquiringly as I plonked myself down beside him and gulped down the remainder of my drink.

"Don't start," I warned him, "I don't need an inferiority complex coming from you as well."

Of course Hugh was a real man and swung me off into a dance and had me laughing within minutes.

How I wished I loved him and not Richard whom I ignored studiously for the rest of the evening. Elisabeth, who was also at the party, told me afterwards that he had drunk himself into oblivion and Mick had carried him home.

CHAPTER THIRTEEN

S arah had hoped and hoped to get engaged at Christmas and was broken-hearted when Ian didn't propose. She moped around Derryrose so pathetically that Jennifer lost patience and resolved to take matters into her own hands.

On her instructions we lured Sarah into the attics to visit Sue the new pup who was sickly. Jennifer in the meantime intercepted Ian at the bottom of the drive, and leaping into the Twin Cam Corolla told him to drive on, as she wanted to talk to him. I should think Ian obeyed without question: Jennifer was a gangster, not a gangster's moll. They had returned within ten minutes and Jennifer came exultantly into the kitchen where Daisy was feeding Sue teaspoonfuls of hot port in an attempt to buck her up a bit.

Daddy had been given Sue by a farmer friend who said that her dam was a first-class sheep dog. As the lineage of her sire was suspect—rumour has it there was a hot-blooded poodle sighted in the neighbour-hood—and as she was the runt of the litter, the farmer was probably lucky that he didn't have to pay daddy to take her away. Daddy naturally was delighted with himself and brought Sue home wrapped in the Aran sweater that mummy had knitted him, wrapped up in his dreams of appearances on *One Man and his Dog.*

Jennifer hadn't divulged her plans to us beforehand or we would have tried to stop her. She revealed all now. She had told Ian quite simply that if he didn't propose to Sarah that very night she was going to leave him.

"Oh I think he believed me," she said airily. "He was eternally grateful. He really likes me you know."

All men liked and admired Jennifer, but they couldn't love her because she wouldn't let them.

Sarah arrived home half an hour after her deadline and woke the house to tell them that she was to be married. Not of course until she had finished teacher training and they had bought a house. (And a fridge and washing machine and dishwasher and matching His'n'Hers pyjamas, Jennifer said somewhat spitefully.) It certainly seemed as if her fate was sealed and we all pretended that we exulted in the idea of having Ian as a relation.

We were digesting an indigestible Christmas dinner and picking through a huge box of Quality Street, given us by our impending brother-in-law Ian, when the phone rang. No one likes answering the phone in Derryrose at the best of times as it is in the hall which has sub-zero temperatures, so the ringing was ignored until mummy said, "Perhaps that is your fiancé, Sarah," and Sarah bolted upright and dashed for the phone, blushing with embarrassment.

Jennifer and I were arguing over who was to have the last purple sweet in the box and Daisy was accompanying us with a dreadful Beethoven Sonata on the piano when Sarah came smashing back into the room and announced, "It's Laura on the phone, and she has some dreadful news."

Mummy and daddy, who had been arguing over whose turn it was to go for sticks for the fire, leapt up and made a simultaneous dash for the telephone. Sarah sat down on the sofa and informed us that Laura was coming home in June with the rest of the American connection to get married.

The telephone is a fair bit away from the sitting room but down the passages I could hear daddy bellowing into the receiver, "I don't believe you."

Daddy wasn't the only one who couldn't believe it. Daisy, Sarah, Jennifer and I forgot it was Christmas Day and retired to the kitchen to hold a council of war. Of course, we had to dissuade Laura from such folly. Living with Lee in sin was all right; it was even romantic in a way—but to marry him? He was

American; even Ian was one-up on that. So we composed her a letter which basically said that though we approved of fornication, we did not wish her to become the wife of the American. We finished the letter:

"We are praying for you Laura that God might reveal to you the error of your ways, that you might even yet be saved from this Hell you are creating for yourself."

Laura didn't even bother replying to our missive. No doubt she thought we were being small-minded Presbyterians. Maybe she was right. Sarah sighed a few times, while we discussed it. I may have been wrong but the sighs weren't altogether of disapproval. But she was engaged, what more did she want?

Trouble had sprung from another corner and we had our hands full enough without worrying about Sarah's sighs. Mummy became possessed with a cleaning demon.

Once upon a time at Derryrose one could set down a book or pen or hairbrush or a piece of soda bread and jam, and return to the object a month later to find it undisturbed, nursing a dainty layer of dust.

Suddenly everything changed and those happy days were no more.

Henry, Brenda and Sue, up till then as familiar about the house as the biped family members, were banished to the great outdoors and met a barrage of abuse when they ventured over the threshold. Everything was tidied away, which was excellent, except that no one knew where it had been tidied to.

Jennifer's only bra disappeared on New Year's Eve and though she searched the usual underwear haunts, like cupboards, drawers and wardrobes, then everywhere else including the cellar and the coal-house it didn't turn up. She left for Dublin complaining bitterly to me that she would be shapeless and sagging by Easter—it never occurred to her to buy another one. I don't understand why she was so distressed, her bra had been grey for many moons and she could have bought a parachute harness-type model in Dunnes Stores for 99p in the sales.

Daisy rescued Jennifer's sagging anatomy by discovering the bra at the end of January in Brenda's outdoor kennel in the corner of the byre. It can only be imagined how the offensive item ended up there, and it made me wonder just what Daisy was up to that she found it. It wasn't only the bra that got tidied away. My novel *The Country Girls* walked from the sitting room, and my latest nail varnish Russian Rhapsody got no further than the kitchen table, vanishing within half an hour of entering the house. Daisy suffered least because she was scatter-brained by nature and couldn't remember where she set things anyway. The fly in the ointment was of course our beloved mamma. She became even more obsessively tidy, and I became quite worried when Daisy wrote to say that the washhand-basin in the bathroom was now scoured every morning and the kitchen floor brushed after every meal. No food could be eaten anywhere but in the kitchen, and the dining room had been papered for the first time since my parents' wedding.

Of course the reason for this upheaval was Donald's and Lee-Ann's impending visit. Mummy disliked many of daddy's relatives, considering them stuffy, conservative, pompous and snotty, yet she was terrified lest any of them think her a slovenly slattern. The American connection in particular had excelled themselves in banking and Lee was the only reject to come from the States bearing the name of Gordon. Laura had returned from her summer with these over-achievers with an exaggerated description of their opulent lifestyle and of the maids who cleaned the colonial mansion twice weekly.

With an army of servants Derryrose might have been a showpiece of Ulster architecture but years of wellie boots and doghairs and uninterested house-keeping had converted the showpiece into a home. Mummy might drive herself and us into an early grave yelling at us to clean up after ourselves and to hoover our bedrooms, but this contrived cleanliness could never capture the glamour of bygone days.

Sarah and I papered the bathroom walls during the Easter holidays, which was good fun as they had been painted white since I had been born and had been flaking since I had been old enough to pull the paint off while bathing. The five of us had often bathed together as children and we had a competition that whoever pulled off the longest flake of paint could sit beside the taps. This was the best seat in the bath as you could run as much hot water into the tub as you liked and the heat remained round you, the other bodies restricting the movement.

We had given up the communal baths when Laura's breasts began to sprout and she was embarrassed by their size at an early age. Certainly they were the biggest breasts I ever encountered on a thirteen-year-old, and I envied the wolf-whistles she got when we were at school because my own breasts never grew to half the size.

Sarah was very quiet the first morning while we stripped the walls. She picked at the flakes of paint and sighed unenthusiastically. I thought the sighing meant that she was missing Ian, who was on an accountancy course for a week, and said so. She flushed at the sound of his name, and sighed more deeply.

"Oh Helen," she had stopped pulling at the flakes of paint completely now. "Oh Helen I know I should be the happiest girl alive, engaged to a man who respects and loves me..." She sighed again.

I sat on the edge of the bath and took her perfectly manicured hand in my own. My hands were bruised with the lambing, and my nails were short and not very clean. Sarah's long white fingers were so beautiful but her diamond engagement ring was cutting into my hand.

"I don't love Ian the way Laura loves Lee."

She watched me nervously. Perhaps she thought I would be shocked or angry with her. Her hands were cold as ice. I didn't speak because I couldn't think of anything sensible to say. If I had been Laura I would have hugged her and said "So he is an incompetent lover after all." But I wasn't Laura so I said nothing.

Taking my silence for encouragement she continued: "That night in Kerry, when we talked about our boyfriends—I can't stop thinking about it. It was the first time I admitted to myself that Ian does have faults. And now we are engaged..."

She was on the verge of tears and I sat mute because tears embarrass me. Jennifer would have said "Screwed?," Daisy "Consummated your love?", I opted for "Slept together?"

She nodded gratefully and the truth came gushing out unchecked like the cold tap on the washhand-basin.

"Helen, it was horrible. I don't know what I expected. I thought maybe it would be poetic or I would hear violins or seagulls screeching."

Oh God I thought, why did she read so many Mills and Boon romances?

She was staring at her diamond ring but I don't think she even saw it.

"When he touched me it was as though he was tuning a wireless set. Press the button and get an immediate response." She smiled glumly and I got the impression that it was a relief telling somebody.

"Did you tell him?"

She opened her eyes wide with surprise.

"Of course not Helen, he would never forgive me. Ian has so much going for him, and does he know it! His ego would never recover from hearing that I could experience more sensitivity in a rogue bull elephant. You know, the more I think about it the more convinced I am that I don't want to marry him."

Courage was blossoming with every sentence. And to think we all considered her spineless.

"You know, we might criticise Laura for being swept away with carnal passion, marrying in haste, throwing her academic successes to the wind and hitching up with a bum but she is happy. Far happier than me with my mortgage savings, Ian's secure job and his prospects. And all because Lee is obviously an awesome lover. I heard her saying once that a well-laid woman can forgive her man anything, and she is right. I think that if you aren't satisfied with the passion in your life you blame everything that goes wrong on your frustration. Ian has irritated me terribly this last month. He has a horrid habit of sucking in and blinking rapidly before he touches me. My flesh is creeping at the thought."

It was as if she was running faster and faster down a mountain path and couldn't stop.

"When are you going to break the engagement?"

She took a deep breath. "When he comes home from the course I'm going to finish with him completely."

She noticed my consternation.

"I have been thinking about it for weeks Helen, so don't give me that. 'Are you sure you know what you are doing?' look. I've been waiting for days to get the opportunity to tell you."

What a transformation from the boring tearful non-human to this gutsy broad. Reading my thoughts she added, "I am a Gordon, Helen. The fire in the rest of you is in me as well but it expresses itself in a different way. I know you are amazed that I can finish so calmly with Ian but it doesn't cost me a thought. Once my mind is made up you know, I don't believe in looking back."

"Then you have the heart of a lion," I congratulated her.

She shook her head. "No, courage isn't being fearless. Courage is being afraid and going on."

Secretly we all rejoiced at the termination of Sarah's engagement. Mummy was the only person to express regret and that was only because Ian had flattered her once by saying she was a lovely woman and looked young enough to be Sarah's sister not her mother. She chastised Sarah for letting a good thing slip away, but when Sarah explained that he was a lousy lover she was somewhat mollified. "I have unblocked toilets with more enjoyable prodding and poking," Sarah said.

Mummy at least appreciated the importance of passion in a marriage, which is why she was so calm about Laura's choice of husband. Only a week before, while we had been painting the skirting boards in the dining room she had said, "There is nothing your father enjoys more than us going out for a Guinness, sharing a bag of fish and chips on the way home and then back for a night of sex."

Because of my exams in Dublin I missed much of the crescendo of excitement which heralded Laura's homecoming. Daisy and Sarah who both went home at weekends said the atmosphere at Derryrose was electric. Jennifer refused to venture northwards until mummy's phase of cleaning passed. She did leave Dublin the Easter weekend in the hope of having an Easter egg bought for her but was greeted at the door step with the words: "That bedroom of yours is a disgrace Jennifer, and you aren't getting a bite of food until I can see the pattern on the carpet."

When I phoned home at the weekend, wedding wedding wedding was all that mummy could talk about. We had decided unanimously years ago to wear mummy's wedding dress and make whatever alterations we fancied ourselves. Jennifer reckoned that by the time she was ready to marry the dress would have been hacked away to nothing and she would have to wear white satin shorts. Laura intended making no alterations and sent instructions home that she wanted all four of us to act as bridesmaids and to decide among ourselves what colour of satin to make our dresses.

It was fortunate that we all had the same colouring and midnight blue was eventually decided on by Sarah, whose taste in these things was vastly superior to the rest of us.

"I know you would have chosen red," she explained to me over the telephone, "and Daisy kept eyeing a chintz pattern that would have made us look like armchairs. I think midnight blue is most suitable in the circumstances."

Jennifer who was blowing smoke rings in the phone box beside me said, "It's Laura who should be wearing whore red."

Laura was voluble with excitement when she got off the plane with Lee on 28 June. She raced into daddy's arms with a very unbridelike squeal of joy. Mummy had threatened to poison daddy before the wedding if he didn't behave himself with Lee and I had been sent to the airport with him to ensure that he did. She remained at home giving everything a last-minute polish, though Donald and Lee-Ann weren't to fly to Ireland for another month. They were having a holiday on the continent while Laura and Lee prepared themselves for the forthcoming nuptials. The wedding date was set for 15 August, and the newly-wedded couple were to spend two weeks' honeymoon touring the Free State before returning to America.

"What did they need a holiday for?" grumbled daddy who would have preferred Laura to spend the two weeks at Derryrose with him. "Their lives are one long honeymoon."

It was a relief to me that Laura was unchanged by America. She was sleeping with me as Lee had been given her bedroom. Mummy said she preferred that they maintain a veneer of respectability while they stayed under her roof.

"Ridiculous," scoffed Laura as we prepared for bed on the first night she was home. "Lee and I have been sleeping together since our first summer. Poor Donald, he used to worry lest Lee take advantage of his sweet Irish cousin. Little did he know. I might have the face of a nun, but that's where the innocence ends."

"You know our values are different from those of the Americans," I argued, slapping Nivea cream on to my face. Sylvia, the Ag college monster, had silken skin which she attributed to the generous feeding she gave her face of Nivea at night. I had tried it too and it had worked.

"Yeah, they have the morals of sewer rats. It's OK to sleep with your boyfriend but when I swore Donald looked at me as if I was Catholic. The Wasps (White Anglo-Saxon Protestants) hate blacks and Jews, and Catholics come a close third."

"And do you want to live in a society like that?" I had finished with the Nivea and was spreading Vaseline on my lips.

"What a mess of stuff you put on your face," said Laura plaiting her hair rapidly in case it stuck to my face in the middle of the night. "None of that American behaviour stuff affects Lee and me. I intend to get fatter on junk food and spend my life riding roller-coasters."

"Are you going to work?" I was now kneeling beside the bed about to say my prayers.

"Oh Helen," Laura threw her hairbrush at me, "You'll be going through the same bedroom routine when you are forty. God help Hugh if he has to kiss you with that muck on your face."

I concluded from that adroit subject change that she and Lee had made no plans for the future. "We plan to be happy," she said.

CHAPTER FOURTEEN

Mummy asked Donald and Lee-Ann to stay about a week before the wedding. They were conducting a short tour of the North at the time, visiting their umpteen relatives. It takes an American to keep contact the way the Irish never do. All our cousins bombarded them with Ulster fare, each trying to outdo the other in their bounteousness. It was probably a relief for them coming to Derryrose, where they could get health-farm treatment, that is, starvation like the rest of us.

I liked Lee-Ann because the first morning she was in the house I heard her yelling at Lee to make sure and brush his teeth. I liked Donald because he told us a story about our grandfather which I didn't know. Granda who had died long before any of us knew him had made his fortune in South Africa before returning to Ireland to marry gran-gran. It seems that on his road to fame and fortune as a young man, he stopped by a cradle and patted the baby's head.

"This," he said, "is the girl I am going to marry."

The baby girl was my grandmother.

The story was probably true because when we cleaned out gran-gran's room after she died we found a pile of letters with South African postmarks. It must have been really odd for gran-gran growing up receiving love-letters from a man that she didn't know, who was old enough to be her father. Each letter ended: "Till I return and you be my bride, God's blessings, fair maid." They were signed "Your Kenneth."

No odder on reflection than daddy taking mummy in exchange for a scrape on his motorcar.

The night before the wedding Laura slept like an angel and I lay awake listening to her snores and contemplating the big step she was taking. Someone had to think about it after all and the bride was bewilderingly unconcerned about the whole thing.

"Does Lee realise you snore?" I had asked her as we lay together in my double bed on the final night of her spinsterhood. A shaft of moonlight lit up her pretty face.

"Of course!" She screwed up her nose and looked fourteen not twenty-four (almost). "He says they are usually tiny ladylike snores unless I have been drinking, then they are as loud as his. He makes a noise like a suffocated bull when he lies on his back but he always stops when I thump him."

I wondered how I would feel if it was me who was

marrying Hugh in the morning. Panic gripped me even at the thought of it. I'd have to be heavily tranquillised to go through with the ceremony. I could imagine daddy taking me up the aisle strapped to a wheelbarrow. Hugh would think the entire thing a huge joke. Nothing I did ever made him cross. I had shifted James Kavanagh, a rather handsome specimen in my class, on the big night out at the end of term and he had simply laughed when I told him. He was so lackadaisical about my fidelity that I had become suspicious as to just what he was up to. I suspected that he had a wife and children stashed away somewhere. Of course he was tickled that I could suspect him of such wickedness.

"Don't you think I have my hands full with you?"

Yes I did.

"But what do you do during the week?" I had persisted, acting like a jealous lover. "I know I occupy you most of the time but I'm not in Belfast during the week."

"I see other girls," he had said, "the way you see other men. But owing to some weakness on my part I still prefer you."

I jumped out of bed and sat on the window seat, arms wrapped round my knees. If Hugh was so good for me, why did I shy from the thought of marrying him? Bloody Richard, of course, I thought, lurking

like a praying mantis in my mind. On the last night
of term he had sat beside me and talked solidly to
Elisabeth about farming, though they both knew that
Elisabeth has no interest in the price of barley. Hardly
any wonder I had shifted James when he left without
saying goodbye to me.

I wished I could sleep as I didn't want to resemble
a wilted lettuce leaf on Laura's big day. Mummy's
wedding dress hung ghostlike in the moonlight from
the top of the wardrobe and I was thankful that it
was Laura and not me who was getting married in
the morning.

Gordons only crawl out of the woodwork for
weddings and funerals. The last time there had been
a family gang-bang had been gran-gran's funeral. I
watched them shaking hands with each other and
exchanging names and professions. Daddy's relatives
fought so much amongst themselves it was a wonder
that they even tried to be civil. Marvellous how a free
feed patches up differences between people.

"Kenneth, doctor," said a bearded man shaking
my hand enthusiastically.

"Helen, bridesmaid," I replied thinking that he
was very like the man who owned the garden centre
in Magherafelt. I had already shaken hands with four
Margarets including Great-aunt Maisie. She had
grasped Hugh's hand—he was standing beside me

looking a bit frightened—and said, "Are you fit for her, young man?"

Before we left for the church mummy sent me to wipe half of my make-up off my face. She said I looked like a factory girl not a bridesmaid. So much for my trying to conceal my sleepless night. The bride was beautiful as she sailed up the aisle on daddy's arm, followed by four very demure bridesmaids—we had been warned that this was not to be the day we made exhibitions of ourselves.

Hugh sitting beside Aunt Maisie got a sharp dig in the ribs from her as I passed their pew. I assume this was to draw attention to me. After the service he said, "That aunt of yours would be after me herself if she was 60 years younger." They hit it off magnificently together and I watched them laughing out of the corner of my eye while the formal photographs were being taken. The turbulent thoughts of the previous night had resulted in a revolting pimple sprouting on my forehead, so Sarah organised my hair so a curl covered it during the photographs. Unconsciously echoing my sentiments she muttered, "There but for the grace of God go I," as Laura and Lee took to the floor to thunderous applause at the dance afterwards. No one had taught either of them to dance and they looked daft smooching to "Lara's Theme" from *Dr Zhivago*. It was mummy's favourite tune, as she and daddy had first seen the film on their honeymoon. Mummy fancied that she looked a bit like Julie Christie as they both had fair hair. It would have required vast quantities of imagination to detect similarities between Omar Sharif and daddy.

"So my dear," said an old uncle of daddy's, "will you be the next to go?" He was whirling Aunt Maisie round to a beat of his own. I blushed because I knew Hugh had heard him and suspected he was waiting to hear my answer. When you are hiding something, always be flippant. I laughed, "Oh God works in mysterious ways, his wonders to perform." Hugh didn't laugh though the old cousin was delighted and pinched my cheek and told me I was a fine wee girl. Hugh presented me with his arm and suggested we go for a stroll in the gardens. When he got me on my own and we were dawdling slowly past a bed of white roses he said, "Helen, I want to marry you some day."

I felt sick and said nothing; yet I continued walking quite calmly beside him.

"I don't want you this year or next year, so you can start breathing again."

His face was lost in a pool of shadow, but his voice was smiling. "Some day," he continued, "when we have both grown up and you have no more conquests to make, then I want to marry you."

He didn't expect an answer so I relaxed.

"Hugh..." I felt humble. "Hugh I don't deserve you."

"I know," he was definitely grinning. "And if you won't take me I shall marry your Great-aunt Maisie instead. You will be exactly like her when you are eighty."

"Aunt Maisie broke her heart over a man who didn't love her."

"Yes," said Hugh, "I know she did."

Because like all silly girls we were fascinated by marriage, and especially by whom we were going to marry, each of us put a piece of wedding cake under our pillows the night after the wedding. One of the Margarets had told us that if we did we would dream of the man we were going to marry.

"Maybe this isn't such a good idea," Sarah mused as we queued for the bathroom to wash before bed. "What if I dream of Ian? I don't want to marry him."

"Or Anto the Onion?" I added. "What if I dream of Anto?"

"What if I don't dream of anybody?" asked Daisy who was taking ages to wash the make-up off her face. "I think I would rather dream of Ian than discover I was to be an old maid."

"Aunt Maisie is a very happy old maid," I said loyally. Maisie was my favourite aunt. I had to defend her.

"No she is not," said Jennifer who though she didn't intend washing had joined us in the bathroom and was eating her piece of cake.

"I'm not going to marry for a long time," she explained, "So I will just leave the marzipan under my pillow."

"About Aunt Maisie," she continued after we had all expressed consternation as to her diminishing marriage prospects, "When I was up in Donegal in July staying with her I asked her why she never married."

"Oh Jennifer," protested Sarah, shocked. "How indelicate!"

"What did she say?" I was not shocked, just interested.

"She said she fell in love with our grandfather the day he arrived back from South Africa to claim gran-gran. She was seventeen at the time and he was the most handsome man she had ever laid eyes on. Tanned and lean, with wild red-gold hair bleached almost white by the sun. She got really carried away telling me about it—it's like it had happened the day before yesterday. It seems according to Aunt Maisie that she and granda were perfect for each other: she was fit for him, and gran-gran never was. She is convinced that he would have carried her off if he hadn't decided to marry gran-gran twenty years before. And you know what we Gordons are like, thick-witted and stubborn to the end. Aunt Maisie says he was such a man, she stressed the man, that he made gran-gran love him. Aunt Maisie said she never loved another man and she never forgave gran-gran for being born first."

None of us could remember what we had dreamed about the next morning except Jennifer who said she dreamed she was being chased by Charlie Montgomery. No matter how fast she ran he kept up and when she shouted at him to go away he didn't hear her. It was a good sign though that she had dreamed about a man at all. She still claimed to abhor and despise Charlie.

The only highlight of my final year in Dublin was the night Jennifer shifted Charlie. For some reason I was at a Vet Society disco and the last I saw of Jennifer she was leaving with him, a wicked gleam in her eyes which I recognised heralded a wild night.

"We are not having a relationship, we are shifting," she told me the next day, because as a concerned sister I insisted she spit it out.

"You are such a nosy wagon, Helen. I thought Michael Hughes had you totally tied up. You didn't look as if you had time to be spying on me."

"Jennifer," I laughed, "I wasn't kissing him, I was

whispering into his mouth and anyway I couldn't help noticing you and Charlie. You looked as if you were going to rip all his clothes off and have your wicked way with him."

"I'm not so sure about this rape business," said Jennifer complacently, inhaling deeply so that I shuddered for her lungs.

"Do you think Daisy is going to hate me for ever? Or is she so satisfied with that karate expert of hers that she will forgive me this lapse in integrity. It is a bit low shifting one's sister's ex-man."

"I'd say she is delighted," I comforted, thinking of the huge smile of "I told you so" on Daisy's face that morning.

Jennifer looked anxious.

"You know I don't like him any better than I ever did, Helen. I still think him a toffee-nosed, self-opinionated pipsqueak but I do have the hots for him. So long as it's just shifting and none of this boyfriend-girlfriend stuff."

Ironically, or perhaps not so ironically, I met Charlie that afternoon in Rathmines. If I hadn't known Charlie's rather blasé attitude towards the female sex I should have even said that he was looking for me, waiting to talk to me. He insisted on treating me to tea, though we hadn't communicated socially since his casting off of Daisy and his plummet into the B category.

"Your sister..." he began.

"Which one?"

He glanced up to see if I was fooling or serious and laughed when he caught my eye. "Them both," he admitted. "I have never met two blood relatives so unlike before. I mean Daisy, bless her, is a sweet scatter-brained butterfly and Jennifer..." He didn't finish. "Jennifer is a demanding, self-opinionated hornet," I finished for him, highly amused at his eloquent turn of speech concerning Daisy. I would tell Daisy and we would consider elevating him from the B category.

"And though you used to love Daisy and hold the memory of those happy innocent days with her sacred, you fancy the pants off Jennifer."

Poor Charlie, he still wasn't sure if I was teasing.

"Jennifer says you are not having a relationship," I added.

"Damn the woman." He was clearly impressed. "Have, have you any advice for me, Helen, please?"

There was thinly veiled anxiety in his voice, just enough to prove that he was a man after all and I forgave him for being a B category.

"Not I," I smiled, "You have made your bed now you must lie in it. But with whom?" I added, saucy like. Then to convince him I was on his side I said,

"Jennifer doesn't want a boyfriend, Charlie; she isn't interested in a relationship. But she says you are a good shift."

His smile was beautiful, I almost fancied him myself.

"Thank you Helen, you always call a spade a spade. Jennifer calls a spade a shovel as you know. Well I don't want a girlfriend either, and she is a good shift if you don't mind me saying so and it seems we understand each other perfectly. How is Richard?"

Oh Hell, first Daisy, now Charlie, catching me off guard.

"I think he is all right," I was guarded where I should have been flippant, "You probably know more about Richard than me Charlie, we don't bother about each other any more. I think he has outgrown me."

Charlie didn't look surprised as I had half hoped he would and he didn't say, "But Richard is crazy about you." He didn't even say, "But you are perfect for each other." He simply laughed at my woebegone expression and patted me on the head as he left. "He is the only man I know who doesn't worship the ground you walk on, Miss Gordon," he said.

I sipped the dregs of my coffee and wondered crossly why life wasn't ever more like Wuthering Heights.

I admit I was disappointed that there was not a

major row the first time Daisy encountered Charlie in the house visiting Jennifer. Daisy met him in the kitchen one morning when she was talking to the kettle.

"I was standing with my back to the door encouraging the kettle to boil faster to fill my hot water bottle," she told me. "I didn't even realise he was in the flat let alone at the kitchen door listening to me raving at the kettle. When I stopped to draw breath he said, 'Daisy Gordon, you never change,' in the voice he told me to buy the Alpen and my heart stopped again the way it did then and I poured the water in the kettle all over the floor and my pyjamas and not into the jar. And he laughed at me and just in the nick of time I remembered what an insensitive horror he is and how he bullied me when we were going out together. It's just as well that he laughed when he did or I might have fallen for him all over again and that would have been grisly. He's very attractive still. I can't stop thinking that he is very attractive."

But whether or not Daisy still found Charlie very attractive his head was turned with Jennifer and the taming of the shrew had begun.

CHAPTER FIFTEEN

When I finished university I had no concrete plans about my future. Throughout my final year I watched my classmates rat-race for management jobs in large companies based in England. I endured endless conversations between hitherto normal girls about their interview suits and the frightening prices they had paid for them. My interview suit had belonged to Aunt Maisie and was made by Chanel in 1942. It was probably quite a cool-looking suit in the '40s and I was very attached to it. I think it was just as well I was never called to interview because it was a little too different for a prospective assistant of an assistant manager. I had no desire to be the monkey in any company so I didn't waste time applying for such positions.

"But what are you going to do?" mummy demanded, frightened that I was going to situate myself in Derryrose and upset her cleanliness regime by leaving coffee cups under my bed.

"You said I could do anything I wanted once I got my degree," I defended myself, "So I am thinking about it."

And I was thinking about it. First I thought of joining an escort agency, then I thought of commercial bee-keeping. Then I thought of joining my uncle in his antique business as he was advertising for an assistant. I finally settled on becoming a novelist. The novel was rather a formidable step to contemplate just then though, what with my jam-making and wine-making and gardening and baby-sitting my parents over the Twelfth. However I felt I had the capacity to write light romance. Heavens I had had enough light romances to know what I was writing about. Words and thoughts and sentences began flitting through my head so I carried a pen and note pad round with me to catch the random literature before I lost it again. As pens that write are like gold dust in Derryrose I kept my biro on a piece of string round my neck. Mummy thought I was mental and scoured the newspapers for suitable employment.

She even resorted to the "What is the matter with you?" talk when her blood pressure soared as the Twelfth approached and daddy became the Supreme Commander again. I remember Jennifer getting a "What is the matter with you?" talk once while I had been at Ag college. Mummy had been holding onto Jennifer's ear at the time yelling, "I am exercising considerable restraint," as Jennifer's ear turned blue.

"Why didn't you take that advisory job the Irish Department of Agriculture offered you?" she asked me during the talk.

"I don't want to live among Papishes any longer," I implored her hoping the Supreme Commander would march in and save me. He did.

"Now Jennifer," he commanded mummy. "Leave our daughter alone. She hasn't even graduated yet. If she is still unemployed in September I shall see what I can do about getting her into the shirt factory. She may be lucky enough to get work as a stitcher."

"And if I am not lucky?" I asked aghast. The Supreme Commander had an alternative sense of humour.

"Tea lady." He roared with laughter as mummy stomped off to vent her blood pressure on Brenda who had never resigned herself to the outdoor life and who was trying to sneak undiscovered into the kitchen. For one so petite mummy has a voice I rarely disobey. Brenda's canine brain didn't appreciate the voice though and I heard mummy emphasise her threats with the floorbrush.

"What about your novel?" daddy whispered in tones of hushed reverence. Military men respect literary genius.

"Progressing," I whispered back though I hadn't progressed beyond scribbling. There was plenty of time to think of a plot. Plots weren't really crucial in light romances. It was the colour of the heroine's eyes and the squareness of the hero's jaw. I was researching the light romance business very thoroughly, reading one of Sarah's Mills and Boon novels daily. I felt there was a gap in the market I could supply. Inspiration, like a shaft of sunlight, would hit me some day concerning the plot.

My graduation was the only bit of excitement I got in July. Mummy had persuaded me to assist in Uncle Billy's antique shop while he took his wife and children to Greece for a month. She hoped being left in charge of the business would make me interested in it. I had enjoyed the first week. I listened to Gerry Anderson on the wireless in the morning, the Archers at lunchtime, *Woman's Hour* in the afternoon and did *The Irish Times* crossword after that. And when inspiration struck I scribbled at my novel.

But at the start of the second week I got a bit of a headache which simply refused to go away. That was the week I was graduating at UCD and Daisy was left in charge for the day I was away. The headache was if anything worse in Dublin and the ceremony had been agony. I attributed the headache to tension, the thought of ignoring Richard at the graduation and the botheration of employment in the antique shop when the weather was so good I could be outside burning pale gold. Mummy had gone through a stage once of working as a doctor's receptionist and felt qualified to diagnose anything. She said the cause of the headache was the fact that I drank too much lemon tea, and the row we had had when my new novel *The Real Charlotte* got tidied away and disappeared completely. She said that in adolescence I had reacted to tension by growing spots but now that I was too old to have pimples the headache substituted.

Daddy said it was my eyesight, and that he had known a man who had had a headache for eight years and the day he got his spectacles changed he had never had a headache again. The girls reckoned on sexual frustration (Jennifer) and a broken heart. (Daisy said this but I pointed out that were my heart broken my chest should ache not my head.) Sarah formed no opinion as she was holidaying with Rev Robinson and family in training for when she took up her post as schoolmarm in September. She felt that if she could control Patience, Hope, Isaac, Joy and Samuel she could handle a class of thirty nine-year-olds. Rachael was expecting another baby which horrified all of us especially mummy who often wondered aloud whether she should advise the minister's wife on contraception.

"You had five kids," we pointed out.

"Oh I was young and foolish, and your father was a nasty beast."

Of all of them only Hugh was concerned lest I was really ill but I pooh-poohed his concern. I didn't want to be sick.

The day after my graduation I blacked out in the antique shop. I had been standing at the top of a step ladder lifting a valuable clock off the wall to show to an interested buyer. I afterwards learned that the man had broken my fall but that the clock was smashed to pieces.

Dear Elisabeth,

It is not my handwriting because I can't write because I am having a brain haemorrhage. Last Friday Jennifer and I had a screaming match because she wouldn't let me wear her embroidered blouse when I let her wear my Boots No 7 lipstick all the time, and a blood vessel burst in my head.

Of course I didn't know that at the time, so I changed into a £3 T-shirt I bought in Wellworths sale. (The T-shirt shrank and faded after the first wash.) I cycled Emily into the shop with the approaching thunder of a headache. My head ached worse in the shop and I had to wear sunglasses, though it was raining outside and my customers must have thought my head was cut. The pain got so bad I thought it was cut too.

It was still sore on Saturday night but I bravely went dancing in Portrush with Daisy. I hadn't been fed in a week, as Hugh doesn't count. I met a nice newspaperman who invited Daisy and me back to his caravan for a cup of tea. A cup of tea was literally all I got because the minute I got out of the caravan I had to dash behind it to be sick. I was sick on the way home, poor Daisy had to stop the car a couple of times, and I was convinced I had contacted listeria food poisoning from the raspberry ruffle ice-cream I ate before the disco. Daisy was sure it was the newspaperman's cigarettes.

I looked and felt pretty grotty during the graduation and didn't stay for the dance, but you must remember I was having a brain haemorrhage at the time. Then on Tuesday I inconveniently fainted at the top of a step ladder in the antique shop and smashed a rather valuable clock.

Anyway I ended up with a shaven head in the emergency ward. I would have been getting the last rites if I had been a Catholic. I am more concerned about my baldness and how cold I will be if I am buried without hair.

Now, do stop crying Elisabeth. I am horribly calm about the entire thing. I do long to be a beautiful corpse and my skin has cleared up

*magnificently in the past few weeks but it's a pity
my sunburn has faded.*

*I must confess now, it's now or never. I never
liked the curry you cooked when we lived together,
I only ate it to spare your feelings. And it was me,
not Mick who broke the glass into the bath and
never removed it. I was always sorry you cut your
bum on it but I never had the nerve to own up.*

*Those are all my confessions. I have been infused
with religious fervour since Rev Robinson visited
earlier. I have also had visitations from the Church
of Ireland reverend or is he a vicar? I can never
remember, and the ministers from the Free
Presbyterian and Baptist and Brethren churches...*

Once I was sure I was going to live I got Laura, who
had written the letter, to post it to Elisabeth. I had
wanted no one to know I was ill until I was recovering,
because a death-bed scene, though the life-blood of
the romantic novelist, would have been too, too
embarrassing for a normal girl.

Laura had flown home the day daddy phoned her
to tell her what had happened.

"He was crying on the phone," she told me. "The
last time he cried was when he heard that Jennifer
was a girl and not a boy."

Everyone knew Laura and Lee had no savings and

I asked her where she had got the money to fly to Ireland at such short notice. She told me to mind my own things but it transpired that she had pawned her wedding ring. "You are my sister," she said.

I didn't really enjoy being the centre of attention when I had a bald head, and I was glad I was in a private room where I was on view to no one. Most of the time I was so drugged I didn't know whether I was coming or going. On the occasions that I was alert enough to dictate letters, and make conversation with my family I usually insisted that someone dab my nose with powder or smear my lips with lipstick. Imperative to keep up appearances even on my death-bed. I was convinced, when I wasn't drugged, that I wasn't going to live. I even had a will made in which I bequeathed my savings to Laura and the wine and jam recipes to Daisy. My family cheered up enough to eat my sweets, read my letters and listened to my earphones when they visited, and I wasn't drugged.

When Elisabeth read the letter she threw up. Then she phoned Derryrose to enquire after me. Then she phoned Richard to tell him, and ask him to take her to the North to see me. Of course Richard didn't know what had happened because I had insisted that no one tell him. I couldn't have borne to have seen him. It would have sent me straight into relapse. When I was drugged I sometimes had nightmares about him. I was concentrating my energies on Hugh who was with me constantly and who would have done anything for me. I suppose it takes a crisis for people to show their real colours.

Richard made no excuse about refusing to come and see me. He simply told Elisabeth that he didn't want to.

My hair grew back pale red gold, totally unlike the shade it had originally been. Initially I had been terrified lest it grew back grey.

"Your hair is not that colour," Aunt May said when she visited.

"Tell it, not me."

Convalescence at Derryrose was a bit of a farce. Theoretically I was supposed to lie-in in the mornings and breakfast in bed, but I was such a light sleeper, and had slept so badly since the illness that the morning sun peeping through my curtains, or Laura scratching herself in the adjoining bedroom were enough to wake me. Sometimes I was glad to be awake because I had terrible dreams. I think it was all the medicine I was on.

I heard the prologue of a dogfight in the bathroom one morning between Laura and Jennifer over who had used the last of the toothpaste and then the imposing interruption by mummy telling them to be quiet immediately.

Laura seemed to be in no rush to return to America and her husband even though I was out of immediate danger. She said she enjoyed being home, that the climate was better, and the people weren't so obvious. They were lame excuses because she didn't give a damn about climate or people as a rule.

"Lee is too laid back to take a lover," she told me as if reading my mind.

September 3

Isn't September the most reassuring month? Summer you love unquestioningly as you love a smiling child but autumn is different, more thoughtful, more mature. The thoughts of autumn are long long thoughts, as if she knows all, understands all.

Today is the morning of my rebirth, back from the jaws of death. There were dew-soaked cobwebs in the orchard today and a soft wind blew into my room this morning whispering, "Get up, get up and live." I went downstairs to find mummy throwing saucepans at daddy and calling him "an interfering old fart," because he suggested that she shouldn't smother the fried bread with so much butter. It isn't really butter of course but Echo margarine: we have run out of the other stuff.

Daddy escaped outside and she confided in me that she thinks he has become anorexic because he has started refusing food she cooks. It would have been heartless to remind her that the bacon was burnt solid. I wonder if my parents' behaviour will continue to bewilder me when I am as old and as married as them?

September 8

Mummy has finally done what she has threatened to do for years. She has had a pay-phone installed in Derryrose. Sarah is devastated and Jennifer suicidal as they spend their lives on the phone though mummy nags constantly and frequently pulls the extension cord out on them. The phone makes a horrible bleeping noise so we can't disguise the fact that it's a pay-phone at all. I think it is quite funny.

I am now writing vigorously at my first light-romance novel, and it becomes easier every day. I think my heroine is going to be struck down with an illness like my own only in her case the love of her life will mount a white charger and storm the citadel to be with her. Light romance overthrows reality. I must write it so I admit it to myself. Richard Knight never came.

September 15

I can't believe this is autumn. A gentle mist lifted this morning to reveal a scorcher of a day. I abandoned my convalescence in favour of a revealing suntop and shorts. Couldn't detect my sunglasses at all so I squint as I write.

Last night mummy and daddy went to a dinner dance to celebrate their wedding anniversary. The dance must have been a success as they were still speaking to each other on Sunday morning. I thought it suspicious that they both stayed at home to "cook dinner," and missed church. By Sunday afternoon mummy was crippled with back pain, so terrible that Daisy made tea and Sarah washed up afterwards.

"It was the jiving," she said. But I have my own theory. Mummy and daddy are too old to relive the fortnight of their honeymoon in one evening now.

At the end of September I did something which I didn't want to do, but which I had to do. I took my copy of Emily's Quest *down from my bookcase and looked at it for a long moment. Then methodically I ripped out all the pages and shredded them into the fireplace. On the top of the funeral pyre I placed a photograph of Richard and me taken at UCD. We were laughing together in the photo so*

I ripped it in half. I didn't want to be burned with him.

I lit the fire with a hand that didn't shake, and watched the flames leap round the laughing man in the photograph. He took a long time to burn but I watched until the laughter was ash.

Richard Knight never came when I was dying.

CHAPTER SIXTEEN

Hugh visited constantly and brought me silly presents to cheer me up. I knew he was thinking a lot about us getting engaged though of course he was making no demands. One day he arrived with a roll of brown paper to "line my bottom drawer," and asked me if Aunt Maisie had given me her tea-set.

Traditionally in our family the bride leaves home with a tea-set. Because it was unthinkable that we would marry before our eighteenth birthdays, the tea-set was chosen and presented as an eighteenth birthday present. Laura, Sarah and Daisy all had their tea-sets on show in the wedding cabinet in the dining room—Laura had never taken hers to America. At the time I was eighteen I hadn't been able to decide what tea-set I preferred and never got round to choosing one. Mummy consequently forgot that I was tea-setless. Jennifer, who had never chosen one either, often said I was never going to catch a husband without a tea-set. Aunt Maisie must have overheard the Great Tea-set Debate because she descended on my convalescent bed one quiet day in September with the hideous one her Sunday school class had given her decades before. Vainly I protested that I didn't deserve such a sacrifice, because I knew her to be inordinately fond of the dreadful thing, but she was adamant.

She brought me a six-pack of Guinness as well to build me up. Mummy considerately removed it lest Rev Robinson see it, and drank the lot herself. So the ghastly tea-set joined the other dowry offerings at the bottom of the wedding cabinet and I started to think that, maybe, marrying Hugh wouldn't be such a bad thing after all.

My first major outing was in September to Ballymena of all places because Daisy wanted to shop in the Tower Centre before going back to Dublin for her final year. She was to live with Jennifer which I thought would be interesting especially if Charlie came calling for a bit of sex and they were sharing a bedroom.

Convalescent stout or not I was pathetically thin and though September is not a cold month I shivered a bit and wore Daisy's green headscarf the entire trip. A drunk once told her she looked like Princess Anne in the headscarf but *he* wasn't bald and ill, and anyway it was no one's business but my own what I covered my head with. I would have looked much sillier in Aunt Maisie's lace skull cap.

Once Daisy had satisfactorily squandered her final dole cheque on an eyebrow comb, a pink pencil-sharpener and a home perm we descended on one of the ancient dress shops littering the town centre to fit on hats before we went home. Hats are mummy's passion and her wardrobe bulges with them. The only time I ever saw her wear one was Laura's wedding. She loves the type with loads of fussy net and feathers and ribbons and became attached to a horrid one sporting all three the minute we entered the shop. Jennifer told her it looked like a mutilated body on the top of her head.

The shop assistant bustled over and rather officiously demanded if she could be of any help. She was one of those old biddies that are kept alive only to antagonise country people in posh shops.

"Are there any other shop girls?" Jennifer asked rudely. You could depend on Jennifer to put an upstart in her place.

"Tell her to take that stupid-looking hat off her head, she looks daft," Jennifer continued jerking the thumb to indicate mummy admiring herself in the head-on-collision hat.

The woman collected herself admirably and sweeping a condescending gaze over my headscarf flounced over to Daisy who was glorious in a huge peach straw creation. It was a pity she was eating ice-cream and had got some of it on the end of her nose. As the best form of defence is attack Daisy launched into a breathless, "Do you think the colour suits me?" before Granny Grumpyhead could say her piece. Daisy then dropped the rest of her ice-cream down her pinafore, and as if in explanation told the shop assistant confidently, "It's the home perm I bought, I'm so excited at the thought of curly hair I can hardly think straight."

She whipped off the hat and dropped it absent-mindedly. "Do you think I will suit curly hair?"

Sarah suddenly felt sorry for the shop assistant and decided it was time we left. She forcibly propelled us from the shop, and insisted that mummy leave back the red hat. "I'll smack you if you buy it," she told mummy.

The primary school teaching had gone to her head.

I had to retire to bed the moment we returned home because I was exhausted, what with the travelling and the constant bickering between the back-seat drivers.

"You aren't indicating," Sarah would start because she drove as if she were a computer and always signalled as if programmed to do so.

"Shut up," Laura would cut in. "Don't disturb her. She is driving too fast as it is. We will all be killed if we go over the hedge at this speed."

Then Daisy would interrupt, "No we won't; we are so tightly squashed in the back seat we won't even move if the car overturns."

Then mummy would start to pick her nose at a road junction and they would all yell at her for being so disgusting though I had witnessed Sarah doing exactly the same thing the day she drove me home from the hospital.

I was bravely swallowing egg flip when Daisy came in to model her new hairstyle. (Eggflip is raw omelette and considered convalescent food in South Derry.) Mummy had permed Daisy's hair and it looked really cool.

"Don't I look different?" she questioned as I pulled the soft ringlets and teased her that she looked like a Presbyterian on Children's Sunday.

Daisy was so successfully curly that Laura and mummy decided to get themselves done as well. Sarah was very tempted but felt that her reputation as a responsible schoolmarm would be shattered if she appeared in P5 covered in curls. Jennifer had shaved her head in sympathy with me after I came out of intensive care and was still bald as an egg.

"What will Lee think of your curls?" I asked Laura that night. She was lying on my bed beside me studying the chessboard.

"Oh Lee," she said in a voice that suggested she

was trying to recall who Lee was. "Oh Lee will never know," she said, carefully studying the black queen.

"Why?" I wasn't sure I wanted to hear this. I had a silly longing to be back in hospital with Hugh stroking my hand and whispering "Wee Pet," protecting me.

"I am leaving him."

Well! This was the last straw.

I shut my mouth which had dropped open.

"Checkmate, Helen honey." She laughed, tipping the chess pieces higgledy-piggledy into their box and snapping the lid shut.

"I am tired of being married."

"But you have only been married for a year," I protested. I would have taken her more seriously if she hadn't smelled so abominably of perming lotion.

"I'm sorry," she said but of course she didn't give a damn.

"Now take that massive scowl off your face, Helen," she said severely, "or you will have another brain haemorrhage."

I had an overwhelming desire to slap her face but I restrained myself in case another vessel did burst and packed her off to get my evening constitutional bottle of stout. While she was away I convinced myself that it was just a phase she was going through. She returned with my stout and a rather healthy glass of gooseberry wine for herself.

"What are you going to do?' I asked quite nicely, determined to be mature about her desertion.

"Well actually," she drank the wine rapidly, "I'm going to have a baby."

Mummy cried when she heard Laura was pregnant because she thought she was too young to be a grandmother. She didn't want to have to wear crimplene dresses after the baby was born.

Sarah, Daisy and I discussed approaching aunthood.

"How marvellous," breathed Daisy. "Bearing a child is the fulfilment of every woman's purpose on earth."

"Don't be so stupid," said Sarah, who had developed feminist tendencies since her split with Ian.

"A woman has the capacity to excel in any field, not just that of Rent-a-Womb. I think she and Lee are the most irresponsible adults I know. How can they bring up a child between them?"

"Well actually," I said quietly pulling the pin from my grenade and plopping it in front of my sisters. "well actually Laura has decided not to go back to America. She prefers to have her child here. In Derryrose, with us," I added just to make sure they understood.

"Oh how wonderful," said Daisy delighted. "A baby here, in Derryrose. We haven't had a baby here since Jennifer was born. I shall start knitting baby clothes immediately."

"God," said Sarah who never swore.

Mummy and daddy were delighted that Laura was staying in Ireland, deserting her husband.

"It's so nice to have your family round you," mummy explained.

Throughout November Laura expanded with child, and after a scan the child became children—she was expecting twins. More delight. I was getting better rapidly and could perform simple tasks such as feeding the ducks and baking apple tarts. As I improved Laura went into decline, so we had a bit of a role reversal, with me waiting on her.

I spent half an afternoon picking the last of the blackberries and the other half baking her a blackberry tart which she loved. However none of my family would eat it because I hadn't strained the worms out first. If I hadn't owned up I don't think they would have ever guessed. Not even Hugh could be duped into eating a piece though I employed every feminine wile I could muster in the attempt. He simply laughed and told me to behave: I was a seductress since my hair had grown back. Hugh had kept laughing through my entire illness though there were times when I knew the laughter was to hide his worry. Sometimes in hospital when he had thought me asleep or so doped I was vegetable I had seen him slumped in the chair by my bed looking old and sad and tired. I tried to tell him that I cared for him, that I couldn't have survived if it hadn't been for his eternal strength, but he had only laughed and told me to straighten my bedcap.

Yet when he asked me to marry him at Christmas I said no.

It had been terribly romantic. We were at the rugby club's dinner dance and I had worn the scarlet dress. My skin was white as porcelain—illness not asses' milk—and I threaded jet beads through my hair. I thought I looked beautiful and Hugh wolf-whistled when he came to get me.

The dance had been a great success and I could have been slightly the worse for the wine when Hugh stopped his car on the way home. I felt rather giddy.

"Are you going to tip my car seat?" I giggled foolishly, noticing for the first time that he had stopped beside the lough and there was a full moon glinting on the water. So silent, so graceful, the moonlight.

We walked slowly hand in hand along the lough shore and the only noise in the stillness was the sound of our footsteps on the shingle beach. I had been thinking that Handel's *Water Music* ought to be playing in the background to complete the effect when he swept me off my feet—literally—and into his arms and grunted, "Helen, you fat heifer, you must weigh five hundredweight."

We both laughed because I was still stick-thin and all angles. I curled up close to him on his knee when we sat on a convenient seat considerately placed by the DOE for courting couples to enjoy the moonlight.

"Helen Helen Helen," he murmured nuzzling my hair and the square of neck exposed above the collar of my coat.

"Hugh Hugh Hugh," I responded. Maybe I was still drunk.

He stopped kissing my neck and cradled me firmly in his arms, tipping me back on his knee so that my face was brightly lit and looked straight into his.

"Will you marry me?"

I opened my mouth to say yes, and I saw happiness break over his face as he anticipated my answer, and then a voice inside my head which wasn't my voice said, "You destroy everything that loves you," and the happiness on Hugh's face exploded, reflecting the expression of my own.

I didn't speak, but of course I didn't have to. Hugh knew. Like a real gentleman he apologised and took me home. "I'm sorry Helen. I thought the time was right. I thought you were ready. I can't help loving you to death."

If I had spoken I would have cried so I said nothing.

Morning found me huddled on my window seat in the bedroom watching dawn break over the lough face but not seeing. Seeing only the look of pain on Hugh's face and remembering Richard's "You destroy everything that loves you."

I had really thought I wanted to marry him, and all my sisters bar Daisy had agreed that he was the man for me.

"None of them appreciate the effect you and Richard Knight have on each other," she explained.

"Oh Daisy," I had argued, "I haven't seen Richard since we graduated." Saying his name made me ache, an old wound. "He didn't come when I was ill and I can't forgive him for it."

"Did you want to see him, Helen?" Huge dark eyes eating into my honesty. "Did you want him there watching you die? You were very ill, you touched death. I wouldn't have wanted him there if I was you."

I had dismissed Daisy at the time. I hated Richard. Glowering reserved Richard. Cremated but not totally dead yet.

I had cried the eyes clean out of my head by the time Laura woke and shouted in at me from her bedroom.

"How did it go, baby? Big night?"

I went into her room, and she, still lying in bed, took one look at me, groaned loudly and said,"You refused Hugh, didn't you?"

I pretended to ignore her, and got into the bed beside her, evening dress and all.

"Stupid girl." She turned her back on me.

"I'm not stupid!"—defiantly.

"So why are you crying?"

So logical, so unperturbed. The type of woman who flew home from America and didn't fly back.

"I suppose you think you are still in love with bloody Richard Knight." Since my illness Laura always prefixed Richard's name with a "bloody."

"Why would you think that?" I was tired, tired of Richard. Tired of wanting him when he didn't want me.

Laura sat up in the bed.

"When you were in intensive care trying to decide whether to live or die I had a bit of a hoke in the top drawer of your dressing table. I knew that was where you kept your cheque book and I hadn't a penny. I reckoned that if you died you would never know." She paused for breath.

"Charming," I said. "What is all this preamble leading to?" If Laura was confessing to embezzlement,

God only knew what she was about to come out with.

"There is a photo of you in the drawer, of you and bloody Richard Knight. You are looking at each other and laughing. It's all intimate and happy."

"That photo was taken years ago," I told her thinking of its ashes in the fireplace, and my violent tears in September over it.

"Helen you don't want Richard bloody Knight. He is a spineless wimp, always was. Fancied the pants off you at college, always too frightened of you to do anything about it. He had a thousand opportunities to shift you, never took one of them. You of all people don't need a wimp like that. You need a real man to keep you in line. And you know as well as me that Hugh is all man. And stop listening to Daisy filling your head with romantic drivel: she is an airhead."

I had crawled under the bedspread because she sounded too convincing.

"You are supposed to be the romantic airhead," I said.

"No," said Laura comfortably, "Just a bit impulsive, that's all."

When mummy heard that I had refused Hugh she yelled that I would never get another man to put up with me the way he did and huffed with me for a week.

Daddy said, "Is Hugh the one with the Toyota car?"

Sarah shook her head and said, "And both of you such physical people."

Even Jennifer was mad with me, though she usually considered herself to be "above all that," because she liked Hugh.

"Helen," she moaned. "He was funny and he bought me cigarettes."

I heard nothing from Hugh and missed him terribly. I found consolation only in my novel which was almost finished. But in it the heroine got her man and lived happily ever after.

CHAPTER SEVENTEEN

I visited Aunt Maisie with my novel in February for her critical assessment. She liked it. "Bubbles," she described it, "It's like bubbles." We were drinking port after dinner on St Valentine's Night and she asked me if I would prefer to be out with Hugh. I hated to tell her that Hugh and I were history because she liked him so much.

"Such a suitable young man," she lamented. "Are you in love with someone else, Helen dear?"

Aunt Maisie was a smart old witch so I told her all about Hugh and Richard and myself. She didn't interrupt while I stumbled through my little story. She smoked her long cigarettes in silence and replaced the Strauss waltz on the gramophone with Pachelbel's Canon in D which she played over and over again hypnotically. When I had finished we sat together sipping the port while the big black marble clock on the fireplace clicked in the silence.

She smiled suddenly and put Vivaldi's *Four Seasons* on the gramophone which I knew was her favourite piece of music and mine too.

"Well my dear," she said, "I don't think you are going to need my tea-set after all."

"What?"

"Because you don't want to be married Helen, do you? You don't want Richard or Hugh or anyone to be your husband; you don't want a husband."

"Every woman wants a husband," I insisted, thinking that she had at last gone senile. Senility could hit you like that, they say. After all Aunt Maisie the happy spinster had loved Granpa Gordon.

"No we don't Helen. I was treacherously in love with Kenneth Gordon when I was seventeen. I considered drowning myself because he wanted Sadie and not me. Of course, I considered drowning Sadie too but I never wanted to marry him. It's one thing being in love, quite another being married. If I was Margaret Gordon I wouldn't be Margaret Adair and I enjoy being Margaret Adair as I suspect you enjoy being Helen Gordon. Traditionally it is much more comfortable to be a couple but it's much more fun being single."

"But I want to be a comfortable couple," I persisted. "I want to go half share in a tea-set, eventually anyway. I just don't know who with."

Aunt Maisie sighed. "You are so stubborn. All you Gordon girls are stubborn, a Kenneth Gordon trait. Richard Knight is the only man you know who didn't let you walk over him. So you wanted him. But Helen, if you had really wanted him you would have got him. You failed once but you would have seduced him again on another occasion. You can get any man you want. Not even Richard Knight is invincible. If you had really wanted him you would have asked for him last summer while you were dying."

"Richard wouldn't come last summer. I told you that. He said he didn't want to come."

"He only said that because you didn't ask for him yourself," Aunt Maisie interrupted impatiently. "All men are the same, they need to be needed. He was probably distraught."

"I have missed Hugh terribly since Christmas," I said to change the subject.

"Of course you do."

Aunt Maisie was in her element I thought sourly.

"If you hadn't missed him, wouldn't that be odder still? Hugh is a delightful young man. Before you told me your story I had hoped you and he would marry. But I never realised, of course, that you indulged in so many flirtations at the same time."

"There have been no flirtations since Christmas."

"Precisely why you have missed him so much."

She was running rings round me. I felt exposed, naked. Self-enlightenment is one thing but enlightenment via a spinster aunt is another. I decided it was time for bed. I kissed her goodnight. She kept very erratic hours, and might decide to sit up all night smoking and listening to Vivaldi. She patted my hand.

"Stay here with me as long as you wish, Helen. I think you have a future as a romantic novelist. Don't dash off and get yourself an unpleasant career because you have no capital. That was the mistake I made. Enjoy yourself when you are young."

I slept dreamlessly for the first time since my illness. My ghosts slept too.

One Saturday in March I was in my room typing my novel with two fingers and Jennifer, who was home for the weekend, was on the window seat, chain-smoking out the window oblivious to all but her own thoughts. I stopped typing and scrutinised her. She had been very quiet all weekend, hadn't started any rows, had voluntarily washed up after lunch. Maybe I thought, maybe she was in love? She certainly appeared to have something on her mind.

"Jennifer," I asked her, "are you in love?"

"No," she continued smoking. "I'm pregnant."

I assumed she was joking so I laughed and said, "Oh that's good. Laura's twins will have a little cousin to play with."

"Yeah," said Jennifer, "I knew you would take it well. How do you think mummy will react? Do you reckon she will kill herself or me?"

"Don't know," doubtfully. Like a wet drip on my neck I suddenly believed her. "Probably you, then herself."

"I'm getting married," said Jennifer. "Charlie insists we get married. He wants to father no bastards he says."

"That's nice." I felt more cheerful. Weddings were cheerful events. "Soon?"

"End of the month, while mummy's wedding dress still fits. Would you like to be my bridesmaid?"

"Delighted."

"Charlie is coming up this evening, and we are going to see Rev Robinson tonight. I phoned his Reverence earlier when I was in Magherafelt. Do you think I should tell mummy now before Charlie gets here?"

"Perhaps." There was no way I was volunteering to accompany her to telling mummy. The thought chilled me.

"As my bridesmaid I think you should be there when I tell mummy, and have a strait-jacket ready for her."

"Are you afraid of her?" I asked.

"Aren't we all?"

Mummy was watching the end of *Gone with the Wind* weeping because Rhett had once again left Scarlett, and knitting at a cardigan for the approaching twins. Pink because she wanted granddaughters.

"Mummy," said Jennifer, "I am getting married at the end of the month."

"You'd better find a husband fast then," said mummy blowing her nose.

"I am marrying Charlie Montgomery who used to shift Daisy. I'm pregnant."

Mummy said nothing so Jennifer went on, "Charlie is driving up from Kerry today, and we are going to see Rev Robinson tonight."

"Well you seem to be organised," said mummy. "Are you wearing white?"

"Yes and Helen is going to be my bridesmaid."

"Charlie Montgomery," said mummy suddenly. "Is he the boy who broke Daisy's heart?"

"Yes," said Jennifer. "He's a vet. He practises in Kerry with his father. After we get married I'm going to Kerry to live with them."

"Does his father know?" mummy was asking the stupidest questions.

"Yes," said Jennifer patiently. "But mummy I'm not going back to the vet college."

"Pity," said mummy. "You would have made a good vet."

Charlie and mummy liked each other. I thought Charlie looked altogether too pleased with himself, given the situation. When I cornered him he confessed,

"I'm just delighted that she agreed to get married. I was sure she would insist on an abortion. You know what she is like."

"But Charlie," stubbornly, "You and Jennifer have never had a relationship. How will you cope married?"

Charlie smiled, "It will be like one long love-affair."

"God," said Sarah when I told her, "why does she have to get married?"

Sarah was really hooked on the feminist business now. She even read the articles in her glossy magazines. I had been shocked to hear her describe Mr Flynn her headmaster as a sexist pig when he called her a "lovely young lady" and addressed her as Miss Gordon. I wasn't really concerned that she thought the quiet little man a chauvinist because Agriculture is rife with chauvinists. If it came to the bit daddy was a chauvinist pig. What did concern me was that she cornered Mr Flynn in his office and aggressively demanded that he refrain from sexually harassing her and refer to her as Ms Gordon in future. Sarah was far too pretty to be a convincing man-hater. I had always visualised feminists as ugly and wrinkled, wearing men's trousers and screaming, "Burn the Bra." Not that any of them required bras—they had nothing to put in them.

No, Sarah informed me, feminism was the doctrine of all free-thinking, intelligent women. Women were not objects to be possessed: their place was not in the kitchen...I thought all the feminist stuff was stirring, women as masters of the universe, but it was water off a duck's back as far as I was concerned. I had conquered the Ag block at UCD, bastion of male chauvinism and I had managed it by acting like a woman, not a sexless counterpart. And Daisy too, who probably thought feminism was a flower, or a composer or a brand of washing-powder had succeeded in Dublin without ever being referred to as Ms. When lecturers called her "young lady" or even "dear" she was flattered. Sarah thought us both traitors to womanhood, and now considered Jennifer the biggest bounder of the lot of us.

"Giving up her career," she stormed to me the day we were in Belfast choosing my bridesmaid dress. "Her brilliant career."

"Good job we aren't blind or we wouldn't see the green man flashing," I said as we crossed the road.

"Helen," she snapped, "that is a green person. It could be a woman wearing tight trousers."

"A flashing feminist," I thought but didn't dare say.

Jennifer and Charlie's wedding took place on April Fool's Day. Because it was shotgun and because the bride insisted, only immediate family was invited. Charlie's father, his grandfather, and his brother

George, who was to act as best man, were the only Montgomerys present. My sisters, my parents and my Great-aunt Maisie completed the bridal party. The Montgomery men had driven from Kerry the day before and had stayed the night in Derryrose so there was none of the tradition concerning bride and groom being separated before the wedding.

"God knows," said Jennifer, "I am unlucky as it is."

1 April was a delightful day and I filled the old house with daffodils and fresh air. Montgomerys and Gordons mingled in the sitting room enjoying a pre-service drink together. I felt more pretty than I had in a long time when the admiring eyes of George Montgomery were upon me. When he talked about Richard I saw no ghost at my shoulder. I spoke of him quite naturally. I didn't stop to wonder if he would appreciate the picture I made in my quiet, long-sleeved bridesmaid's dress.

Aunt Maisie was flirting with Charlie's grandfather.

"Are there no women in your family?" she asked him.

"They can't survive us," he replied winking at her. She laughed. "Oh, you will have bother getting shot of my niece Jennifer," she said. "The blood of a strong breed of woman pumps the Gordon heart."

Charlie looked a little shook I thought, though I

suspected the root was not matrimony but the Bush whiskey daddy was liberally dispensing. He had been chatting to Laura who was massively pregnant, swollen and bloated, and who had been advising him to lock Jennifer away when she grew as large and ugly as herself.

"Radiance in pregnancy is a myth," said Laura wanly. She did not look well.

"Where," asked Charlie, "is my bride?"

I had sent Daisy upstairs to keep Jennifer company while she dressed and to keep an eye on her in case she did anything unexpected. You could never trust Jennifer to behave just as you could never be sure of daddy. Daddy would have to be removed from the whiskey bottle which he was sharing with Charlie's father. They were discussing Twin Lamb Disease. I excused myself and made for the kitchen to fetch mummy, the only person who could successfully and tactfully get between daddy, the whiskey bottle and pontification on sheep.

Mummy and Sarah were to prepare the wedding lunch but when I got to the kitchen it was Daisy and mummy completing the final touches. Sarah was in the dining room setting the table with the best silver.

"Who is upstairs with Jennifer?" I asked Daisy, forgetting that my mission to the kitchen was to alert mummy to rescue Charlie's father from daddy and

Twin Lamb Disease.

"Oh Helen, I completely forgot about her," Daisy was flustered and scatty, but I couldn't be cross with her. It had to be hard for her, watching the great love of her life take a younger sister up the aisle.

Forgetting daddy I exited the kitchen at speed and up two flights of stairs to Jennifer's room in record time, long dress and all. As feared, Jennifer was unsupervised. She had drunk a bottle of gooseberry wine and was lying naked on the bedroom floor talking to a riding boot.

"Jennifer!"

She craned her neck, staring up at me.

"Helen," she said, "the Lady Helen. Please come in and meet my riding boot."

"You are drunk, you mad eejit," but I didn't feel cross. How could anyone feel cross with a lump of naked flesh. I confiscated the bottle and the riding boot, and uncovered the tin of Andrews Liver Salts she kept stashed away for emergencies. Charlie had given her a bunch of flowers the day before and they were arranged in a pint glass on her cluttered dressing table. I tipped the flowers out and knocked some Andrews into the water stirring it with the stalk of a pink carnation.

"Drink it," I commanded. Once drunk I refilled the pint glass with the water in her wash jug, more

Andrews, and she obediently drank that too.

"No more," she giggled lifting the pink carnation from the bedspread and sticking it behind her ear. "No more water, Helen. I'll be a good girl now. I'm getting married today."

I dressed her. Some perverted streak in Jennifer made her insist on wearing a black lace bra and black stockings beneath mummy's white satin dress.

"'Fuck-me' underwear," she told me as I struggled with the clips on her suspender belt and she swayed unsteadily.

"Virginal to the eye of the beholder, a tart in the flesh."

I nipped down to my bedroom for a packet of mints and when I reappeared she was climbing out of her bedroom window on to the roof. I hauled her back in and force-fed her some mints.

"But the sun is shining," she protested, "and we always sunbathe on the roof."

"Not clad in 'Fuck-me' underwear we don't."

She looked rather pretty in white satin, with her fair hair pinned up and Charlie's mother's pearls at her throat. No one would have guessed she was totally trolleyed. I was arranging her veil when mummy came into the bedroom.

"Mummy," said Jennifer, "I'm sorry if this comes as a shock to you, but I will not be requiring the wedding-night talk on sex. I don't enjoy lying still and thinking of England: active participation is much more fun."

"Getting caught is not," said mummy drily, but she wasn't at all cross. In fact she was rather proud of Jennifer snaring a man of Charlie's pedigree.

During the service, just after Rev Robinson had pronounced them man and wife and Charlie was giving his wife a rather unvirginal snog Laura stood up pale as death, eyes huge, and announced to the congregation.

"My waters have just broken. Could someone take me to the hospital please?"

"God," said Sarah loudly, forgetting she was in a temple of Christianity.

CHAPTER EIGHTEEN

The bridal lunch was a bit of an anticlimax. Daddy insisted on remaining at the hospital with his darling and mummy, torn between her duty as hostess, and her concern about childbirth, fussed abominably. Sarah was of course magnificent and it was only because of her organisation that we got fed at all. While Daisy dithered, and I made abstract conversation with the Montgomery men Sarah efficiently waited the table and mobilised resources. The Montgomery men had marvellous appetites. How was Jennifer going to feed them? One girl—for Jennifer, although expecting a baby, couldn't be described as a woman—one girl in a household of hard-bitten men.

Oh well, if anyone was fit for them, it was Jennifer.

Jennifer and Charlie mysteriously disappeared between the main course—duck—and the pudding which was banana custard and the bride's favourite. Sarah and I telegraphed glances which said, "Could they not have waited until the cake was cut?"

They returned rather rumpled and laughing and

giving no explanation. Mummy was in such a twist about Laura I don't think she even noticed.

The wedding cake was chocolate with Smarties as decoration because Charlie disliked fruit cake and it was only over coffee afterwards that the dreadful truth hit me—Jennifer had no tea-set. No dowry. Horrified with realisation I consulted Daisy.

"What will we do? She can't leave home with no tea-set to take with her."

Daisy looked at me as if I had produced a white rabbit from the cleavage of my bridesmaid dress.

"I shouldn't think it matters," she said, "Jennifer doesn't drink tea."

After lunch Aunt Maisie took Charlie's grandfather out to the gardens for a walk and the rest of us retired to the sitting room.

"How much are you on?" the bride whispered loudly. "How much, Helen, that she shifts him?"

"You must stop drinking," I reprimanded her prudishly. "Your baby will be brain-damaged."

George laughed and laughed when I told him the story of the night I had tried to seduce Richard and he had spanked me. It was a funny story after all. I could even laugh at the past.

"Richard was always conventional," George said, "even at school. Our beds were beside each other in the dormitory so I knew him as well as anyone knows him. I don't think anyone really knows him."

"No," I said. "He is a cold fish."

"Not cold," George corrected me, smiling, "frightened."

I wondered if it would be in poor taste for the bridesmaid to shift the best man while her sister was in labour.

The hall telephone suddenly shrieked and for the first time ever there was a mad dash to answer it.

Mummy snatched the receiver from Sarah and blanched terribly. It was daddy. Laura was having complications.

"Must go," said mummy as if in a dream, "Must go, complications."

In the end we all went, piled precariously in the Morris. Aunt Maisie remained at home to entertain the Montgomery men and because there wasn't enough room in the car, Jennifer and her husband, the latest family member, followed in Charlie's big family Volvo, which, I noticed, still had wellie boots in the back of her.

We made a colourful procession in the maternity ward. The bridegroom and bridesmaid marching up and down the corridor, unable to sit still, the bride pregnant and chain-smoking, Daisy and Sarah on their knees in fervent prayer, mummy sick with fear holding daddy's hand telling him everything was going to be alright.

A nightmare of waiting.

Once, Sarah got off her knees and organised tea for all of us. The biscuit I ate felt like wood shavings in my mouth. I didn't even try to pray. I told Charlie funny stories about Laura and me growing up and especially about the time she fell in love with Reverend Robinson. I think he thought me very in control. Since the time I had been sick I could hide emotion, simply block it out. We sat with Jennifer who was rather green and gulping tea as if her life depended on it. Not the ebullient Jennifer at all.

"Do you think I will be complicated?" she asked Charlie.

"You are always complicated," he comforted her. I left them to be married together.

Laura gave birth to a girl and a boy. All three of them survived though both doctor and midwife said afterwards that it was a miracle. The mother insisted that her family be with her the minute after the birth. We all kissed her in turn. She looked pretty awful.

"Never, never ever again," she said. "Never. Damn you mummy for not warning me beforehand. I begged them to knock me out, but they wouldn't listen. Jennifer, get Charlie to knock you rotten beforehand, it was absolute agony."

Once she knew she was an aunt, Jennifer took

Charlie home to reconsummate their marriage vows and we tried to think of names for the twins.

"A boy and a girl," mused Daisy. "Would she call them Laura and Lee?"

"Of course not," Sarah and I disagreed, "she will probably call them Jennifer and Kenneth for mummy and daddy, especially as she went into labour when Jennifer was being married."

"Scarlett and Shaun," said Laura the next day when we visited. Daisy and I had scoured Magherafelt for the most massive box of chocolates that we could find for her and Sarah was somewhat concealed by the bouquet she had brought. Jennifer and Charlie had not emerged from the marriage-bed at lunch time so we didn't like disturbing them for the afternoon visiting. They could visit in the evening.

The rigours of the previous day had passed from Laura, she was perky and proud of herself, scoffing the chocolates, happy.

"My children are to be called Helen Scarlett and Kenneth Shaun Gordon." She visibly swelled with pride when she said "my children."

"But Shaun is a Catholic name," I said. "Daddy will have a breakdown."

"Helen, you bigot. Shaun is being named for the only real man I know, Shaun Thornton, the Quiet Man," and suddenly I remembered that she had a husband.

"Lee," I said, shocked. I had forgotten him completely.

"I don't want to call my son Lee," said Laura.

"Lee is your husband," I reminded her, because she had obviously completely forgotten about him too.

"No he is not my husband." She was quite firm. "I am married to him but he is not my husband. He doesn't know about the babies. Why should I tell him? They are my children, not his."

"Laura is quite right," said Sarah, because I had a look on my face that suggested I did not agree and Sarah was a feminist and feminists didn't believe that men had feelings. All men were B category.

"Perhaps Lee would like to see your children," said Daisy quietly. She had been bending over the twin incubators since we had arrived, totally engrossed in the tiny lives inside. She had cried her eyes out the night before because the whole thing was so beautiful.

"Of course he doesn't want to see them," Laura comforted us. "Helen..."

She took my hand. I knew she wanted me to understand.

"Real life is not a romantic novel, Helen. Lee is a man, not a hero. And I don't love him. I love you, my family. My children are your children, not his."

She added: "You should be flattered, baby, not cross. Scarlett is yours. I want her to be as wanton as you used to be. The way you were at UCD, when no man was safe. You have to train her to be a sexy beast."

I smiled but I felt tearful. Laura hurt me saying that. It hurt because it was true. I wasn't a sexy beast any more. If I had been a sexy beast I would have shifted George Montgomery yesterday in the shrubbery after the wedding.

It was sad really. I knew how to be but I just didn't do it any more.

Daddy huffed and puffed dreadfully over the name Shaun.

"Never been an Orangeman called Shaun yet," he said and thenceforth always called his grandson John.

My nephew and niece were christened on the first Sunday in June. Having been born prematurely and lived in incubators for the first six weeks of their lives the fuss made of them when they first came home was obscene. Mummy lined Scarlett's cradle in pink frills and Shaun's in blue. Scarlett was given a huge pink teddy bear, Shaun a blue one. Sarah snorted but said nothing. Already we could discern personality traits in them. My little namesake was precocious and demanding and cried all the time, while her brother was the quiet man.

"Daisy was a quiet baby," mummy mused, "but even she cried when I stuck a nappy-pin in her."

Laura and her children moved in to the big nursery bedroom Daisy and Sarah had shared so, on the toss of a tenpenny-piece I acquired a room-mate—Sarah, and Daisy took over and Laura Ashley-fied Laura's room.

Aunt Maisie visited for the christening but there wasn't even word from the newly-weds to say whether or not they were travelling up from Kerry for the event. So Aunt Maisie slept in Jennifer's room which was directly above the nursery, and after a particularly noisy night of Scarlett I caught her trying to smother her great-niece with the pink teddy bear. I rescued my aunt and marched her off to the orchard before breakfast to calm her down.

"Dear Aunt M," I consoled her, "Scarlett is a tiny baby, and she has had a trying life so far. Hospital incubators and Laura for a mother. You and I would both howl. She doesn't even realise she is crying."

"Of course she knows she is crying," sulked Aunt Maisie. "That nasty infant is the image of my sister Sadie and she winged and girned like that all her life. There weren't any tears in the brat's eyes. She was yelling for attention."

"Well, Shaun is a very good baby," I said.

"And he *should* be crying," said Aunt Maisie

peevishly. "What is the point of being a man if you are so bird-mouthed that you can't even cry for yourself?"

Laura joined us for breakfast, with Scarlett under one arm, wrapped like baby Jesus in a swaddling tablecloth she had been given as a wedding present. I wondered if Jesus had presented Mary with nappies as vile as Scarlett gave us. Sometimes Laura changed her wearing rubber gloves.

"Take your screaming niece," Laura commanded dumping the noisy bundle on top of me. Poor girl she didn't look her best after consecutive sleepless nights. I hoped for the baby's own sake that she would settle down soon. If her mother didn't wrap her in newspapers and hide her in a dustbin, Aunt Maisie would drown her.

"Motherhood would be wonderful," said Laura pouring herself a cup of tea, "If there were no babies."

Scarlett stopped crying when I took her into the sitting room stuck my finger in the decanter of port and gave it to her to suck. I didn't like to suggest that Laura keep the child permanently inebriated in case she took me up on it.

"You have such a way with her," Laura encouraged when I returned to the kitchen with Scarlett smiling drunkenly at me. "I'll give her to you for your birthday if you like."

Keeping Scarlett and Aunt Maisie apart was not the only cross I had to bear. Sarah showed the classic symptom of a sexually frustrated woman—she was fanatically tidy and aggressively neat. The fact that she made our bed every morning hardly compensated for her tendency to sweep my belongings off the floor and into the wardrobe or to throw a wobbly if I left a hair-grip on the bedside table.

I slept badly as a rule and, since summer had come, usually woke with the dawn. Alone in my room I would fling the curtains back and open the windows and type at my novel. With Sarah there I had to lie tossing quietly until sheer desperation compelled me to rise and sneak outdoors. It was on my return from one of these early morning rambles that I had encountered Aunt Maisie murdering Scarlett.

Sexual frustration is a frightening disease. Thankfully it is not contagious. Sarah dusted the bedroom with a zeal resembling religious fervour, and cleaned the windows which was the most unloved of all domestic tasks at Derryrose as the frames were rotten and crumbled away when touched.

She went too far when she threw out the vase of dried grasses in the fireplace and arranged my bookcase alphabetically.

Originally each of my books—which were loved as family members—had their own positions on the shelves and when I wanted one I knew exactly where to find it. I had placed them where I thought they would be comfortable with each other. Stylish wit, such as Evelyn Waugh and PG Wodehouse rubbed shoulders on the top row, while sturdy reads by Dickens and Hardy preached from the lowest shelf. I felt physically unwell when I saw my volume of Wilfred Owen's war poetry propped against *Montgomery, Field Marshal, An Ulster Tribute*.

And then the correction pen I used to erase typing errors disappeared and Sarah denied even seeing it. I searched the bottom of the wardrobe; I searched outside in case it had fallen from the window sill while she was cleaning; I looked under the bed which was where anything that was lost appeared.

No correction pen.

I pulled all the bedclothes off her in the middle of the night and revenge was sweet. Next morning I found the correction pen in the bathroom cabinet.

"That's not Tipp-Ex," Sarah scoffed, "it's tooth-paste."

Helen Scarlett Gordon was baptised into the Presbyterian Church in Ireland borne in the arms of her Aunt Helen. Her mother held Kenneth Shaun Gordon during the service and both babies behaved impeccably. What no one realised was that Helen Scarlett was possibly the only Presbyterian ever to be baptised under the influence of alcohol. Laura, my family and my Aunt Maisie in particular congratulated me on my unique ability to soothe her. I accepted their praise with grace and dignity but did not reveal the secret of my magic touch.

Sarah bought the twins a phallic-shaped cactus plant as a christening present and I thought this was the last straw.

"Sarah," I said, "You need a man."

"Certainly not," said Sarah. "I don't need a man and I don't want a man."

And she intensified her cleaning operations accordingly.

CHAPTER NINETEEN

Mummy and daddy decided to go on holiday that summer to celebrate the fact that they had survived each other for twenty-seven years.

"We had thought of waiting until we were married thirty years," mummy explained, "but I might have divorced him by then."

"And I might have died from a lashing from her tongue."

I never understood why daddy said such things because we all knew as sure as eggs were eggs that mummy would huff. It was that time of year again, the season of the Supreme Commander.

"The next time round," said daddy, "I am going to marry a woman who doesn't answer back."

They glared at each other, spoilt children lost for a smacking.

To break the tension I asked, "Are you going to treat it as a second honeymoon?" and was gratified to see them suddenly smile shyly at each other, the eruption of the previous moment forgotten.

"I hope not," said mummy suddenly, "Laura was

conceived on our first honeymoon, bit of an accident you know."

"Yes," daddy agreed grinding his teeth painfully as Scarlett tuned up for yet another session. "More of a mistake than we realised at the time."

Now my parents loved their grandchildren, of course they did, but they were in unvoiced agreement, they would love them more from a distance.

Hence the holiday which was to commence at the start of August and continue "as long as is necessary." I could imagine daddy holidaying permanently until Scarlett grew up. Not that he had ever been on holiday before, honeymoon excepted. We Gordons had a deprived childhood, our summers composed of day trips to Portstewart, and the ritual stay with Aunt Maisie.

There was no plan concerning the holiday.

"A mystery tour," Sarah said when we discussed it, "Mummy is subjecting herself to a mystery tour as a second honeymoon."

She was dusting behind the pictures in the dining room at the time, Daisy was making a flower picture with fuchsias and I was trying to bring up Shaun's wind—he was much too well-mannered to belch in company. Laura had been evicted from this scene of domestic tranquillity with her screaming daughter. Mystery tours were the bogy-man of our childhood.

The forthcoming threat of a mystery tour struck fear into the heart of even the staunchest Gordon. Daddy driving, mummy co-pilot, and us bickering in the backseat of the Morris—what a delightful way to spend Sunday afternoon.

Usually mummy, who was too short-sighted to see the signposts until we were past them and too vain to wear spectacles, gave the wrong directions. And invariably we ended up miles from our destination with all of us dying to use a loo and mummy and daddy arguing over who had fluffed up.

The day we set off for the Ulster-American Folk Park in Omagh and ended up in Derry city they came to blows.

"Of course it's bloody Derry," daddy roared. "Aren't these Derry's bloody walls?"

"Don't swear in front of our children," mummy had screamed back, magnificently. She always seemed twice her height when she was throwing a wobbly, and a halo of light surrounded her. We watched her, enthralled, desperation for the loo forgotten.

Daddy opened his mouth to say something else and mummy punched him on the nose. Sarah gasped, Daisy paled, and Jennifer, devoid of any sense, giggled as daddy toppled backwards and hit the grass verge, supine.

Dead utter silence.

Daisy's little hand in mine was moist with terror.

"Kenneth..." mummy squeaked, "Kenneth, have I killed you?"

We held a collective breath.

Daddy started to laugh. He was definitely laughing. He wasn't dead after all. We breathed. He laughed and laughed and leaping up encircled mummy, tiny again, in a bear hug and hugged her and laughed.

Like a row of five little Indians we padded behind a hawthorn bush to relieve ourselves.

"If she had killed him," Daisy asked me, "would we be orphans?"

"Oh yes," Laura the oracle of all knowledge told us, "Yes we would because she would have been hanged from her neck until she was dead like they did in the wild west."

"No," I disagreed, "they would have chopped her head off."

"I'm glad she didn't kill him," Jennifer contributed decisively, "We would have been sent to the workhouse. The workhouse is much worse than daddy."

I tried rattling Shaun, then bouncing him on my knee but he refused to bring up his wind.

"Men," said Sarah, exasperated, watching me. She had finished dusting and was organising the tea-sets in the wedding cabinet. "Give him to me," she commanded, "I shall bring up his wind."

Such confidence I thought, such a capable sister. While she rubbed Shaun's back Sarah told us she had enrolled to take a car mechanics course over the summer.

"Woman are at a disadvantage in the world of mechanisation," she informed us. "When a car tyre goes flat, what do we do? We wait for a man to fix it. Daisy, stop smirking, you are the worst offender, because you know everything about tractor maintenance yet you would allow any man, regardless of how incompetent he is to do it instead of you."

"True, true," said Daisy, "Men like to feel masterful. I like men to like to feel masterful. They treat me better when I don't compete with them."

Shaun suddenly brought his wind up over the cardigan Daisy had taken such pains to knit him.

"Typical man," we all said together, laughing.

As was their wont before any expedition more demanding than church on Sunday, mummy and daddy rose at six the morning they left home for their holidays. Mummy had had hardly any sleep the night before fretting about leaving us. She compiled an exhausting list of instructions and said that every time she was on the verge of sleep yet another critical item would dash into her head. Rather than risk forgetting it she got up to add it to the list. Daddy, on the other hand, assumed that two daughters with Ag Sci degrees could be trusted on the farm and left it at that.

For indeed, Daisy had graduated with a magnificent degree. Unfortunately, in true Gordon tradition she had no intention of exploiting it to its full potential. I suspect mummy was waiting until she returned, refreshed from her holiday before bombarding Daisy with the "What's the matter with you?" talk.

Since the publication of my novel I was at least established as a novelist in her mind; she even admitted, in a moment of weakness that she enjoyed it. Mummy thought praise made children conceited.

Chain Reaction had been accepted by the first publishing house I had sent it to and I was flattered that they had asked me to send them more of my work. I got a cheap thrill every time I saw it on bookshelves and not so cheap a thrill when money started arriving. Jennifer deigned to write to confirm that the book had survived the perilous trip to Tralee. It was our first communication with her since her migration to Kerry.

"There it was," she scribbled, "Large as life with a whole stand to itself. Of course I didn't buy it but I read it in the shop. Awful trash, but rather readable. I liked the bit where Louise Juliet drops a flower pot on the nerd's head. Girl had spunk, even if she was blonde. But why did you call the hero Hubert? Is it not the most dreadful name?"

The Morris pulled out of Derryrose and extravagant peace descended. Finally released from mummy's enforced regime of domesticity I brought Henry into the house and we shared breakfast in bed.

Such decadence. Daisy pulled a boiler suit over her pyjamas to milk the cows, and while dirty dishes piled high in the kitchen sink we lay naked on the roof sunbathing all morning. We had wine with lunch, and Laura, when she finally rolled out of bed, watched television all afternoon with the twins.

"Square eyes," Sarah scolded, "they will get square eyes," when she noticed all three engrossed in the evening re-run of *Neighbours*.

But Sarah, though she did try, could not stem the outpouring of holiday atmosphere pervading the old house. Her tidying alone could not compete with us all. She retreated to her room to study the instructions sheet and brood on the apparent anarchy we riotously exhibited.

"Old biddy," said Laura when she refused to dine with us that evening. We had gone to quite a bit of bother to have a celebratory meal together. Chips and beans are not adventurous in the gastronomic sense: it was the united front we presented which counted, not the cuisine.

Yet we could not toast freedom without Sarah.

Daisy pushed away her ice-cream without finishing it.

"I can't eat it with a clear conscience," she announced to nobody in particular. "Poor Sarah, it's not her fault if she feels responsibility, some people are afflicted like that."

"She was always too good," Laura growled, Laura who had no problem eating because she had no conscience.

There was a silence and Scarlett decided this was an opportune moment to have her say. She started to cry.

"I'll take her up some tea," I said finally. Laura shot me a dirty look with "Scab" written on it, but I ignored her.

"And I'm going to promise her that we will behave in future," I added firmly.

"Oh, Helen." Daisy's conscience didn't stretch that far. Laura was openly disgusted.

"Compromise," she suggested. "It may be the work of the devil but it's better than good behaviour. Tell her we will wash up after ourselves if she ignores the dogs being in the house. And that we won't sunbathe naked again if we can eat in the sitting room and have breakfast in bed."

Sarah was staring into space when, after a timid

knock I went into her room. Mutually we had decided not to share, conflict of personality and all that, so she had taken over Jennifer's room. I shuddered a little in the aseptic atmosphere.

"We are sorry," I said setting my posy of flowers on the bed beside her. We had no peace pipe. "We aren't going to be bad any more, not even Laura."

"You have been very naughty," she said primly ignoring the posy. "Mummy and daddy weren't away from Derryrose five minutes and you had Henry back in bed with you. And no one washed up after breakfast, and Daisy left her Sugar Puffs swimming in milk and you were drunk at lunch. Yes you were, Helen! And Laura hasn't changed out of her nightdress all day. What if someone had called? What if Rev Robinson had decided to visit?"

Her voice trembled. That was a good sign, she was giving in. "What if he had called? Our reputations would have been totally ruined."

Poor little Sarah, she carried her conscience and her reputation on a ball and chain around her neck, frustration imprinted on her forehead.

"Forgive," I grovelled. "Forgive and we will be good." I considered licking her feet but it didn't come to that. Sarah was too sweet to sulk for the sake of it.

"Promise?"

"We promise."

How sincere I sounded.

Mummy secretly harbours the hope that we are wild young things and phoned one night hoping to catch us indulging in a drunken orgy.

"I hope you are behaving," she said, and you could hear the disappointment in her voice when we said we were. Unanimously we had decided not to tell her that Sue had eaten the patchwork quilt in Daisy's bedroom, and that Sarah had dropped and smashed the Royal Doulton figurine "Sara" that was to be included in her dowry. As none of us was making any shape at marrying mummy had included a Royal Doulton ornament for each of us in our dowries. She hoped it would encourage us to approach matrimony.

"Never," Sarah said at the time. I was starting to believe her too.

We didn't want to worry mummy about the quilt, as she sounded as if she was having a smashing time, and anyway we were repatching it with pieces of matching cotton. A search in the attics had revealed some old sundresses and things which were cut up to use as material.

"It's not the same," Daisy moaned.

"Of course it isn't," Sarah snapped. "Granny Gordon made that quilt forty years ago; that stupid dog managed to ruin it in as many seconds. What on earth was she doing in your bed."

"Don't blame Sue," Daisy protested. "How was she to know the difference between an antique bedspread and a horse blanket. She has been outside for so long she thinks she is a wild animal. And anyway, why aren't you learning something of value at your classes, your sewing is abominable."

Sarah was only mad because she had to replace the Sara figurine. She shouldn't have been dusting it, it was clean. We had no sympathy for her. Sarah didn't know that the dogs slept with us. Sue slept with Daisy, and better than any alarm clock woke her for the early morning milking. Daisy had originally tried to wake to Radio 4, and set the radio alarm clock for 6am. Both she and I, in the adjoining room, were startled to death when at 6am "Rule Britannia" blasted at us.

"I thought we had been invaded," she told me afterwards.

Sue licking her face was a less stressful alternative. Sue had the cows rounded up by the gate by the time Daisy had scalded herself on a cup of tea and struggled into her boiler suit, invariably over her pyjamas. Daddy had resigned himself to the fact that Sue considered herself a cattle dog and not a sheep dog. She disregarded the ewes as if they were nothing more than fluffs of cloud.

As I was a bad sleeper and an early riser I had

offered to do the morning milking for Daisy. Milking parlours have an atmosphere conducive to thought and I was plotting my next novel, a sequel to *Chain Reaction*.

Daisy shook her head when I suggested it. We were in the parlour at the time. I had brought her a bunch of wild roses I had found on my morning ramble and she sniffed their heady scent appreciatively.

"No Helen, no thanks. The farming is my job."

"No it's not," I said in a half-hearted way. "I have an agriculture degree too; I should help you."

I didn't want to, I wanted to concentrate on Louise Juliet and her exploits.

"Helen you are the artist of our little community. We are like a kibbutz here, with mummy and daddy gone. You are the artist, Sarah is the breadwinner and Laura is the mother. And I," she added firmly, "I am the farmer."

I left her to it because I had a sneaking suspicion that she enjoyed being the farmer.

CHAPTER TWENTY

M y suspicions were correct. Daisy was the farmer. She organised farm work with a dexterity lacking in every other task she had ever approached. Like a machine she rose in the morning to the milking and continued full throttle throughout the day, unheeding of assistance. When she stopped to feed, her brain fermented plans and schemes which she bounced off me for consultation.

"A sheep dip," she announced over dinner.

I had had a tedious day with Louise Juliet who though she was married to the delightful Hubert, was considering an affair with the dashing Sir Cecil. Naughty girl. Sir Cecil, for all his money, had buck teeth, and perhaps bad breath. I couldn't let her defile herself with him, yet, stubbornly, she insisted.

"Yes," I said, "a sheep dip."

"I want to build one." Breathless, as if I was going to switch her off, or pull out her batteries at any moment she stampeded through her plans. I half listened.

"Bottom of the far yards...that nice builder will do

it cheaply...depth and volumetric assessment...Helen, I don't think you are devoting your entire attention to the matter at hand."

"Daisy darling," I said, "You graduated third in your class, so I assume you passed the courses on Accounts, Management and Buildings. I trust your judgement."

"Your enthusiasm." Daisy was hurt. "I might ask a little more of your enthusiasm."

"Louise Juliet has been hot-headed and stubborn all day," I explained. "The silly girl insists on running off with Sir Cecil even though he has buck teeth, and an in-grown toe nail. Nothing I write will persuade her otherwise."

"You can't really beat fresh Brussels sprouts," said Sarah suddenly. "I don't care what anyone says freezing vegetables ruins their texture, don't you think so?"

I was listening to Gerry Anderson on Radio Ulster, ironing, turning a duck egg in the frying pan and shouting at Henry to get off the sofa one morning when I heard the door bell clang. The kitchen was pandemonium because Sarah had gone into the primary school to organise something for the forthcoming year, I hoped it was no one important as I dashed to open it. Sarah would have a hernia. The front door sticks because the only time it is opened is to let the minister in, and to let the dead out: we always carry coffins out the front door as a mark of respect. Henry was doing his guard-dog bit round my heels when I eventually wrenched it open.

It was Richard.

If I had been a Victorian damsel or Louise Juliet I would have fainted dead away. But I was Helen Gordon and she had too many ghosts to faint at the sight of one. I told Henry to go back into the kitchen and said, "Richard how are you?" as if I had seen him yesterday and we were friends. We weren't friends. We weren't anything.

"Good morning, Helen."

"Why don't you come in?" I said. I acted the wonderful hostess. I felt as if I was having a dream.

The kitchen was an awful mess. The wireless was blaring, "Donald where's your trousers," Henry was chewing a cushion and I had set the iron face-down on the ironing board by accident and had burnt a hole in a linen pillow case of mummy's. It had been a wedding present. Mummy would murder me when she came home.

I switched Gerry off, scolded Henry and realised I was still wearing wellie boots. Daisy had needed a hand earlier. Could Richard have picked a worse moment to turn up? Why couldn't he have walked in on me while I was painting china or embroidering a handkerchief? I wasn't even wearing make-up.

I could think of nothing to say to him. All I could think was "What the Hell is he doing here?"

He was standing in front of the range ignoring my fry which was cinder black, his hands behind his back, looking at me. I didn't meet his eye.

"Do sit down," I said sweetly. I didn't like to ask him what he wanted. It would have been impolite.

"I was just about to have my ten o'clock tea," I said, "Would you like a cup?"

"No thank you." He was impossible but of course he never had social graces. He had spanked me once.

"Well you won't mind if I help myself then," I said tartly.

"No, not at all."

He continued standing by the range so I left the fry to char and poured my tea. I sat down on the sofa and noticed that it was covered in dog hairs. No wonder Richard had preferred to stand.

"You had that cup when we were at UCD," he said. He was looking at the china mug which had been a present when I was two years old. It had a painting of a yellow duck on the front. I always drank my tea from that china cup. Always had and always would.

"Are you drinking lemon tea?"

"Yes I am," I said airily. "I never change," I added

because I knew that was what he was thinking. Then I wished I hadn't said it because I had changed. I was a hundred years older than when I had last seen him.

He stopped looking at me, and looked out of the window into the yard instead.

"Have you sold all your lambs yet, Helen?"

"No," I answered. I had spent the morning loading lambs into a neighbour's trailer with Daisy. She was at the market with them. Richard wasn't really listening to me, I thought, so I switched Gerry back on. And asked, "Richard, can you dry dishes?"

"Yes."

So I handed him a dishcloth and cleared the table, and washed the breakfast dishes, in my wellie boots, and he dried them and we listened to Gerry Anderson and didn't make any more conversation.

"Have you any pressing farming to do today?"

"I have the milking to do this evening, if Daisy isn't back."

"Anything else?"

I had promised Daisy I would paint a gate, and tighten the fan belt on the tractor. I had promised Sarah I would hoover the stairs and make dinner. I had promised Laura I would call her so she didn't miss the morning run of *Neighbours*.

"No," I said.

"I am going to a house clearance in Dungannon,"

he said. "I believe there are a number of first editions among the books. Would you like to come with me?"

I took my wellies off and went with him. So what? I thought as we drove out through the gates of Derryrose. If I was having a dream it had gone well so far.

"How did you hear about the auction?" I asked eventually, as we sat at the traffic lights in Cookstown.

"My cousin taught in Dungannon Royal," he said. "It's his house."

If houses do reflect the personalities of those who live in them, I reckoned that Richard's cousin had read much and entertained little—like Richard himself. He ignored me completely and devoured the shelves of books in the library. I trod softly through the half-empty rooms and thought empty thoughts. Richard and I had spent hours in book shops in Dublin when we were students and friends...My novel was in those book shops now. I wondered if he realised that.

I was staring out of a high Georgian window when Richard came into the room, and handed me two slim navy volumes.

"Does Lamb still make you laugh?"

The Essays of Elia, and *The Last Essays of Elia*. I opened them with reverence. Excellent condition. He was giving them to me.

"They aren't first editions," he said, apologising for his generosity.

We had tea in a tea-shop in the centre of the town. We had always frequented tea-shops in Dublin too. Once in the course of the conversation I almost laughed but I stopped myself in time. One does not laugh while lunching with a ghost.

"Shall we go?"

We drove home in silence, companionable silence I thought.

Derryrose was in uproar when we returned. Laura in a gaping negligee she had bought for her wedding night was ignoring a screaming Scarlett and was changing Shaun's nappy on the kitchen table. Scarlett's face was scarlet and screwed up. An ugly baby I thought lifting her. She stopped crying immediately. Spoiled too.

Laura didn't look up from Shaun's bare bum.

"Helen," she said, "Why didn't you call us for *Neighbours*? Scarlett has cried all afternoon because she missed it."

Then she saw Richard, bloody Richard Knight. I hoped she wasn't going to be rude. "Laura," I said. Her breasts were very obvious in the thinness of her negligee. "Laura, you remember Richard."

Laura said, "Yes. Hell, what are you doing here?"

Smoothly Richard said, "Laura, after all this time—

good afternoon," or something like that. Laura glared at him, then at me.

"Daisy is home," she said to me ignoring Bloody Richard. "She got a good price for the lambs. She went to do the milking since you were off gallivanting." Finishing Shaun's nappy, she dumped him in Richard's arms.

"Hold Shaun," she commanded, hitching her negligee a little higher on her breasts. "And feed him. Please," she added as an afterthought.

I don't think Richard had ever held a baby before. He looked ridiculous.

"I have business to conduct," Laura informed us, heading out of the kitchen towards the back door. Through the kitchen window we watched her, wellie boot bound, her negligee hoisted above her knees, cutting a straight path to the milking parlour. No doubt to alert Daisy so they could run Bloody Richard out of the house together.

Richard was getting the knack of motherhood when Sarah arrived home fresh from the classroom. She stopped on the threshold of the kitchen, looked at Richard, then at me.

"God," she said.

I introduced them. This is very funny I thought I am going to laugh about this tomorrow. Sarah opened her mouth to say something. Then she remembered she had been brought up to act like a lady. She remembered her conscience and her reputation. "Good afternoon," she said. "Hasn't the weather been dreadful all day? Let me relieve you of that infant, Richard, he has finished his bottle. He must be ready for a sleep. I'll just take him to his pram."

She relieved me of Scarlett in the same way, talking small-talk, a continuous monologue through the entire operation. Magnificent. Then she exited towards the milking parlour in the wake of Laura. I could imagine the three of them standing there, conferring. Would it be pitchforks, or dogs?

Richard decided it was time to leave. He got up and left, didn't say goodbye.

I went upstairs and positioned Charles Lamb between *Some Irish Yesterdays* and *Bricks and Flowers*.

Then I remembered something. In our whoring and touring days Laura and I had kept lists of our conquests, all the men we had shifted. I rummaged about in the bottom of the wardrobe and uncovered an exercise book.

The first entry was devoted to an Austin Holland. I had been severe.

Name: Austin Holland.
Occupation: Mechanic.
Lives: Far away (+1).
Physically: short legs (1) moustache (1) red hair,

hairy chest (-1) massive hands (+1).
Clothes: Farah trousers (-1) White socks (-1)
necklace (-1) striped shirt (-1)
Personality: didn't have one (-1)
Shift: Tried to swallow me (-5)
Comments: Never again.

I leafed to the back of the book to an empty page and wrote:

Name: Richard Knight.
Lives: Don't know.
Physically: Lean, mean, rarely smiles, the right height when I wear high shoes.
Clothes: Never noticed.
Personality: Obscure.
Shift: Never got the chance.
Comments: Have never spent the day with a ghost before.